REGENTS·PARK

Queen Elizabeth Olympic Park

STRATFORD STATION

THE TATE GALLERY
by Tube

IN

oyster

GENERAL

Santander

MW00355877

UNDERGROUND

GANTS HILL

PUBLIC SUBWAY

LONDON BY DESIGN

the iconic transport designs that shaped our city

1 3 5 7 9 10 8 6 4 2

Ebury Press, an imprint of Ebury Publishing,
20 Vauxhall Bridge Road,
London SW1V 2SA

Ebury Publishing is part of the Penguin Random House group of companies
whose addresses can be found at global.penguinrandomhouse.com

Penguin
Random House
UK

London Transport Museum has asserted its right to be identified as the author
of this Work in accordance with the Copyright, Designs and Patents Act 1988

As an educational charity, London Transport Museum works with over 125,000
young people each year, equipping them with skills and confidence to play a
successful role in society.

First published by Ebury Press in 2016

www.penguin.co.uk

A CIP catalogue record for this book is available from the British Library

ISBN 9781785034121

Printed and bound in Italy by L.E.G.O S.p.A

LONDON BY DESIGN

the iconic transport designs that shaped our city

CONTENTS

FOREWORD

London is the world's greatest city. Transport for London (TfL) is responsible for the London Underground network (or Tube, as it is popularly known), buses, rail, tram, river services, taxis, cycling and major roads throughout the metropolitan area.

TfL serves the needs of 8.6 million people and its success depends on constantly investing in its networks to offer the best travel opportunities for all its customers. The modernisation work on the Tube has seen nearly 200 new S stock trains introduced to Metropolitan, Circle, District, and Hammersmith & City lines. Modern trains, signalling and track work on the Victoria line have resulted in a significant increase in capacity. Substantial expansion of some of our busiest Tube stations will add much needed capacity and improved facilities. On our fully accessible bus network, new vehicles are diesel-electric powered, which reduces emissions considerably. New Overground services, Cycle Superhighways and other improvements across all our networks continue apace.

Future developments include the Crossrail route (a high frequency, high capacity service, running from west to east across the city and linking 40 stations) due to open from late 2018, operating as the Elizabeth line. New extensions are planned to the Metropolitan and Northern lines. London Overground will progressively take over the operation of more of London's suburban railway services, and there will be more and more electric buses on London's streets.

Central to all this activity to enhance customer experience is great design. Since the unified London Transport was formed in 1933, it has been recognised that a carefully designed environment is also essential to efficient and functional operations. Not only does great design tie together every aspect of transport across London, it also should perform beautifully in every practical and aesthetic detail. With an ever more complex city and diverse population, Transport for London, as London Transport's successor, continues to demonstrate that commitment to superb physical and digital design is a key priority. Every journey matters, and brilliant design matters too.

This book is an important part of TfL's 'Transported by Design' celebrations, and elegantly highlights the public's choice of their favourite transport designs from past to present. I commend their amazing variety.

MIKE BROWN MVO
Commissioner, Transport for London

INTRODUCTION

The great thing about London's public transport system is that high quality design has been applied to keeping the city moving for more than a century. The consistent application of Frank Pick's 'fit for purpose' design philosophy across signage, vehicles, architecture, maps, posters and street furniture now forms not only the brand of Transport for London, but also of London itself.

Many of the individual designs are regarded as iconic — not precious or devotional in the sense of religious icons, but as 'worthy of veneration', the best examples of applied design in their field. The Tube map, the roundel sign, the Routemasters old and new, the Johnston font, the black cab … each has iconic status, and is venerated and emulated around the world. The title of this book reflects how unique London is among world cities.

London's transport design is so familiar as to be hidden in plain sight to those who use it every day. But when an icon comes under threat or is replaced, the strong emotional pride Londoners have in their city bubbles to the surface; the last day of the Routemaster, the disappearance of the Thames from the Underground map, or the day the Circle line stopped running in a circle!

The Transported by Design festival celebrates how the design philosophy established and evolved by Pick from early in the 20th century has formed so much that is familiar and characteristic in our city. Effective design demands a clear purpose and passionate concern from the client about its fitness for that purpose. The commissioning of good design is crucial to both products and services, for Oyster, the Journey Planner and the management of the London Olympics, as much as for the stations of Charles Holden, the Jubilee Line Extension (JLE) or the humble bus stop. How past, present and future design has formed and moved London and its citizens is featured in a rich exhibition, named 'designology', at London Transport Museum in 2016.

The design icons featured in this book have been voted upon by Londoners to produce a top 10. Many of these icons can be seen at London Transport Museum in the 'London by Design' gallery, at the Museum Depot and out on the transport network. They are distinguished by their incredible variety, their effectiveness and, in many cases, remarkable longevity. They are the stage set and the enablers of this remarkable and vibrant city.

SAM MULLINS
Director, London Transport Museum

CURATOR'S NOTES WERE WRITTEN BY

London Transport Museum

Elizabeth Scott, Head Curator; Simon Murphy, Curator;
Michael Walton, Head of Trading; and Caroline Warhurst, Librarian.

With contributions from Transport for London

Chris Bonner, Senior Stations Strategy Manager; Louise Coysh,
Senior Curator, Art on the Underground; Ann Gavaghan, Design
and Communities Manager; Jon Hodges, Asset Development
Sponsor; Jon Hunter, Head of Design; Eleanor Pinfield,
Head of Art on the Underground.

DESIGNED BY

Sau-Fun Mo, Head of Design, Presentation & Environment,
London Transport Museum.

Quotes are drawn from comments made by the public and TfL
staff about the 100 greatest transport design icons, as part of
a vote on the TfL website and Tumblr, in 2015.

NOTES FOR THE READER

Each entry in this book includes a quote from a member of the public who nominated the icon, information from a curator about the design, details about where the icon can be seen, and a note when further information is available at the back of the book.

Many of the icons are located at the London Transport Museum or the Museum's Depot at Acton in west London, and travel information for these places appears below rather than being repeated in each entry.

TRAVEL INFORMATION

London Transport Museum, Covent Garden Piazza
London WC2E 7BB

For opening times and the latest information about exhibitions, events and heritage vehicle outings, see: ltmuseum.co.uk

By bus: 1, 4, 6, 9, 11, 13, 15, 23, 26, 59, 68, 76, 87, 91, 139, 168, 171, 172, 176, 188, 243, 341, 521, RV1
By Tube: Covent Garden

Museum Depot, Museum Way
118–120 Gunnersbury Lane, London W3 9BQ

Open for monthly guided tours, as well as a number of open weekends each year.

By bus: E3
By Tube: Acton Town
For other travel information visit: tfl.gov.uk/journey planner

WHAT MAKES IT SPECIAL

'The design of the black cab is a truly iconic representation of London.'

CURATOR'S NOTES

London's black cabs are one of the city's most distinctive and comfortable forms of transport. The vehicles are subject to strict regulation, are wheelchair accessible, and have the ability to 'turn on a sixpence'. Drivers have to pass rigorous 'Knowledge of London' examinations before they can pick up their first passenger. This involves memorising thousands of streets, routes and places of interest.

Although known as 'black cabs', these days they come in a variety of colours. You can hail one of the capital's 22,000 taxis in the street, book by phone or app, or pick one up at hundreds of taxi ranks. Be ready for a chat, since London's 'cabbies' are also famous for their ability to talk on any topic.

WHERE TO SEE IT

The TX1/2 type cab (in service 1997–present day) can be seen on London's roads.

London Transport Museum
The FX4 type cab, 1958
(pictured far right)

See also CAPTIONS TO IMAGES on pages 218–220

9
Hammersmith
Knightsbridge
Charing Cross
MORTLAKE GARAGE
Don't ask a man to drink and drive
Don't ask a man to drink and drive
pandora cakes
KENT
HAMMERSMITH
535 CYV

'As the man who commissioned artists, architects and designers for London's transport operators, Frank Pick was one of the most influential people in 20th-century British design.'

CURATOR'S NOTES

Frank Pick (1878–1941) joined the Underground in 1906. He inherited a chaotic Victorian transport design environment and began to address it by applying consistent design standards across the growing system. He commissioned a network of artists and designers, who together changed the face of transport in London.

Pick believed that good design could bring order, style and efficiency, and even a spiritual dimension, to everything an organisation did. The roundel, Johnston font, modern publicity and posters, and Charles Holden stations remain as evidence of his approach. No other modern design programme has been implemented with such effective and comprehensive results as Pick's ground-breaking work for the Underground and London Transport over more than 30 years.

WHERE TO SEE IT

Frank Pick's legacy is everywhere on TfL's systems, and a great collection is at the London Transport Museum.

See also CAPTIONS TO IMAGES on pages 218–220

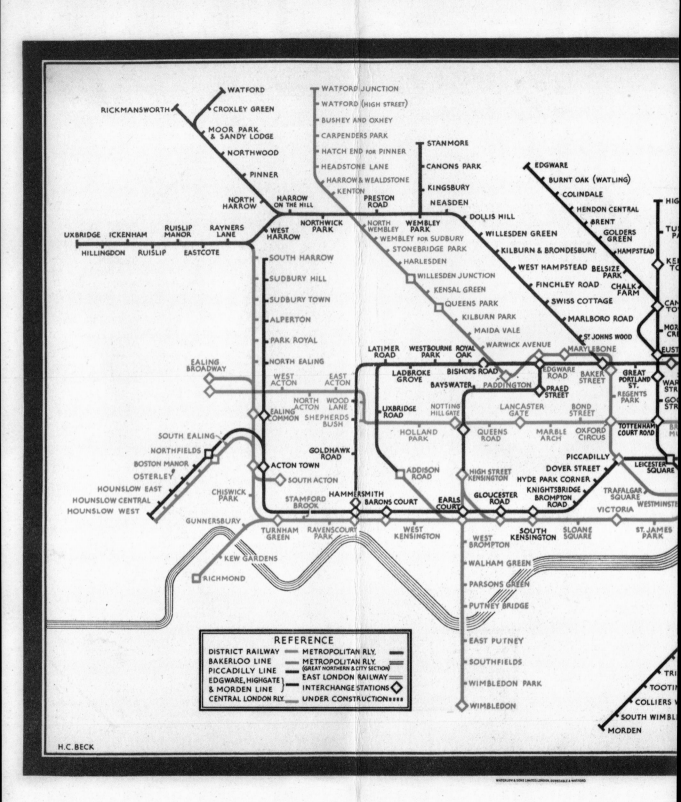

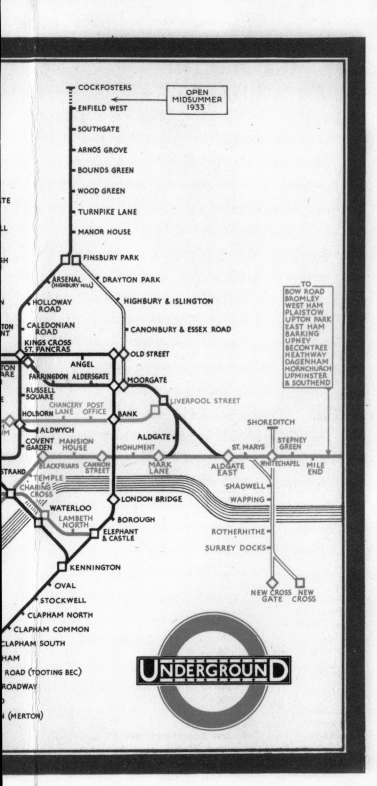

'It is impossible to improve upon … it is beautiful and functional, and because of this it can truly be described as a design classic.'

CURATOR'S NOTES

The London Underground map is arguably the most famous map in the world. It was devised in 1931 by Henry Beck (known as Harry), a draughtsman who worked for the Underground. His diagrammatic map, first issued to the public in January 1933, represented a radical departure from the geographic style of previous maps. Combining functionality with a beautiful simplicity, it is recognised as a landmark achievement in the history of design.

WHERE TO SEE IT

London Transport Museum

WHAT MAKES IT SPECIAL

'The earliest Metropolitan line platforms at Baker Street retain much of their original look and feel from the days of steam. They are still fit for purpose today, and are a reminder of how well some of our earliest designs have held up through our history.'

CURATOR'S NOTES

Designed by Chief Engineer Sir John Fowler, Baker Street was one of only three of the original Metropolitan stations to have subterranean platforms. The dim platform lighting and noxious atmosphere were partly alleviated by the incorporation of skylights doubling as ventilation shafts.

Modified over time, in the 1980s the platforms were restored to their Victorian appearance by stripping the walls back to the original brickwork, exposing the ventilation recesses, and installing replica period furniture and lighting.

WHERE TO SEE IT

Baker Street station (platforms 5 and 6)
By bus: 2, 13, 18, 27, 30, 74, 82, 113, 139, 189, 205, 274, 453
By Tube: Baker Street

See also CAPTIONS TO IMAGES on pages 218–220

WHAT MAKES IT SPECIAL

'It is rare for an organisation to have a device associated with it that becomes instantly recognisable just about worldwide …'

CURATOR'S NOTES

The roundel, or bullseye as it used to be called, is one of the most recognised and familiar elements of Transport for London's corporate identity. First used by the Underground Group in 1908, it has since undergone many changes and been used in many different ways. It now represents all the transport modes in London, and even without any text, it is understood as the symbol of London's transport, and of London itself.

WHERE TO SEE IT

Current roundels can be seen everywhere in London.

Museum Depot

See also CAPTIONS TO IMAGES on pages 218–220

'The Routemaster bus is a brilliant design that has sunk deeply into the British psyche as an emblem of Britishness and of London in particular … it was a design icon long before people started talking of such things!'

CURATOR'S NOTES

Bill Durrant, London Transport's Chief Mechanical Engineer (Road Services), oversaw the team that developed the Routemaster. Every detail of the bus, inside and out, was beautifully designed. Douglas Scott was brought in as an external consultant to work on the body styling, including the front-end design, interior colour scheme and tartan moquette seating fabric.

WHERE TO SEE IT

Classic heritage Routemaster buses are in service on route 15, between Trafalgar Square and Tower Hill.

London Transport Museum

See also CAPTIONS TO IMAGES on pages 218–220

WHAT MAKES IT SPECIAL

'These simple black and white designs look the same at first glance, but each one is different – just like our stations.'

CURATOR'S NOTES

To celebrate the 150th anniversary of the Tube, Art on the Underground commissioned Mark Wallinger, a leading UK artist, to create a new artwork. The result was a major multi-part work that was installed in every one of the Underground's 270 stations.

Each artwork bears a unique circular labyrinth, but with a bold black, white and red graphic common to all. The circular labyrinth echoes the Tube's roundel logo, and the artworks are produced in vitreous enamel, a material commonly used for Underground signs.

A red X marks the entrance of each labyrinth, prompting passengers to enter the pathway and trace the route into the centre and back out again, which is reminiscent of passengers' journeys on the Tube.

WHERE TO SEE IT

See individually designed artworks at every Underground station.

See also CAPTIONS TO IMAGES on pages 218–220

WHAT MAKES IT SPECIAL

Apart from fitness for purpose in terms of both engineering and construction, the RT design is restrained yet familiar and comfortable. It evokes both the city the buses served and the confidence of the organisation that commissioned, designed and operated them.'

CURATOR'S NOTES

The RT type bus was designed in the 1930s, with some 151 buses being produced between 1939 and 1941. Improved design after the Second World War saw mass production from 1947 until 1954, by which time nearly 7,000 buses had been built by AEC and Leyland, giving London Transport the largest standardised bus fleet in the world.

Engineered to meet the rigours of London's traffic conditions and with beautifully styled bodywork, the RT is for many the definitive London bus, being backed up by nearly 50 years of continuous research and development into bus design by London Transport and its predecessors. The RT even became a film star, featuring in the 1963 film *Summer Holiday*, starring Cliff Richard. The last RTs were withdrawn from service in London in 1979.

WHERE TO SEE IT

London Transport Museum
Museum Depot

See also CAPTIONS TO IMAGES on pages 218–220

WHAT MAKES IT SPECIAL

'I chose the S stock Tube train because it is well air-conditioned and looks very futuristic from the exterior. It is very spacious, so it's never too crowded. Also the open-plan interior is quite cool, allowing you to walk from one end of the Tube to the other.'

CURATOR'S NOTES

The S stock, manufactured by Bombardier in Derby, is based on a design originally developed for Movia in Copenhagen, but customised by London Underground. There are two variants with slightly different seating arrangements, designated S7 (seven-car trains) and S8 (eight-car trains, on the Metropolitan line only). Both types have air-conditioning and improved accessibility.

New trains (191 in total) have been replacing older stock from the 1960s and 1970s on the Circle, Hammersmith & City, and Metropolitan lines since 2010, finishing with the last of the D78 stock on the District line in 2016.

WHERE TO SEE IT

By Tube: All trains on the Circle, Metropolitan, Hammersmith & City, and some District line services

09 S STOCK TRAINS, 2010

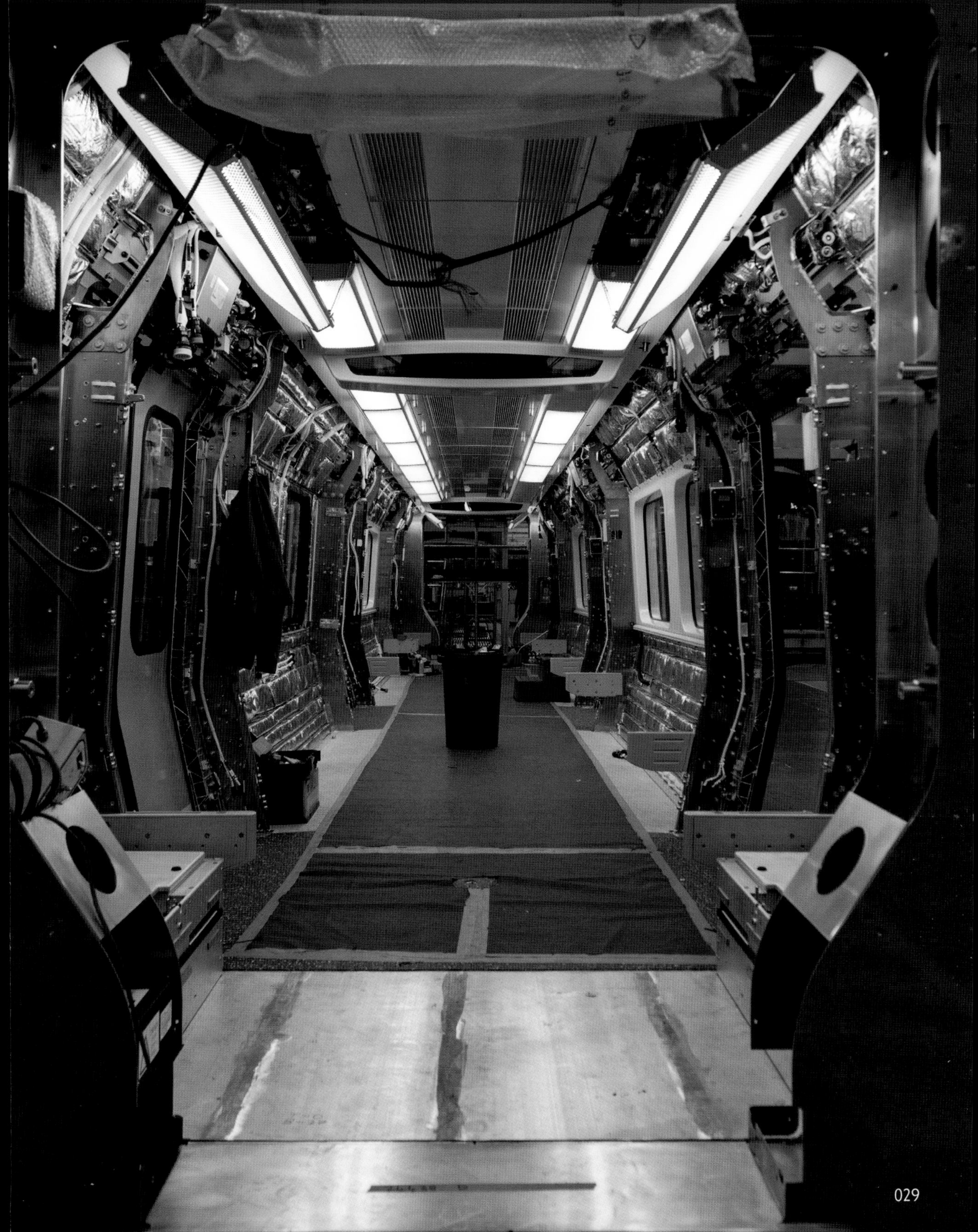

WHAT MAKES IT SPECIAL

'I go through Westminster station on a regular basis and never tire of being wowed by the sheer scale of the architecture. A modern classic.'

CURATOR'S NOTES

Westminster station was the biggest and most complex project of the 11 Jubilee Line Extension (JLE) sites. It involved the complete reconstruction of the District line station while remaining in service, and the construction of Portcullis House above.

The architectural approach taken by the designers, Michael Hopkins and Partners, was to reveal and highlight the engineering aesthetics created to accommodate the difficult site. With the station's proximity to Elizabeth Tower (Big Ben) and the River Thames, and the tight location, part of the solution was to construct a large escalator hall 39m (130ft) deep from surface to platform level. Filled with stacks of escalators and steel supports, it is a breath-taking space.

The station design has won several awards, including the RIBA Award for Architecture in 2001.

WHERE TO SEE IT

Westminster station
By bus: 3, 11, 12, 24, 53, 87, 88, 148, 159, 211, 453
By Tube: Westminster

*'It is both bold and subtle –
balanced and visually pleasing …'*

CURATOR'S NOTES

Frank Pick commissioned the calligrapher
Edward Johnston to design a clear,
modern typeface for the Underground
Group. The innovative result, introduced
in 1916, was inspired by the proportions
of classical Roman lettering, based on
square and circular forms.

Often referred to as 'London's
handwriting', the Johnston typeface
influenced the design of the whole
London transport system. It is still seen
every day, in an adapted form called New
Johnston, by millions of passengers on
signs, posters, leaflets and maps.

WHERE TO SEE IT

Everywhere on Transport for
London's network

London Transport Museum

Museum Depot

WAY OUT

WHAT MAKES IT SPECIAL

'The central staircase and lighting at St John's Wood station is a wonderful example of successful design being more than just physical ... the stunning lamps create a peaceful ambience that is just as strong today as it was when it was unveiled. It is impossible to feel anything but calm. No small achievement considering the number of people who pass through this station every day.'

CURATOR'S NOTES

St John's Wood station was designed by London Transport's Chief Architect Stanley Heaps, and opened in November 1939. The brass uplighters were similar to Charles Holden's designs on the Piccadilly line. The station transferred from the Bakerloo to the new Jubilee line in 1979 and was progressively refurbished in the 1990s.

WHERE TO SEE IT

St John's Wood station
By bus: 13, 46, 82, 113, 187
By Tube: St John's Wood

TOTTENHAM COURT ROAD STATION MOSAICS, 1986

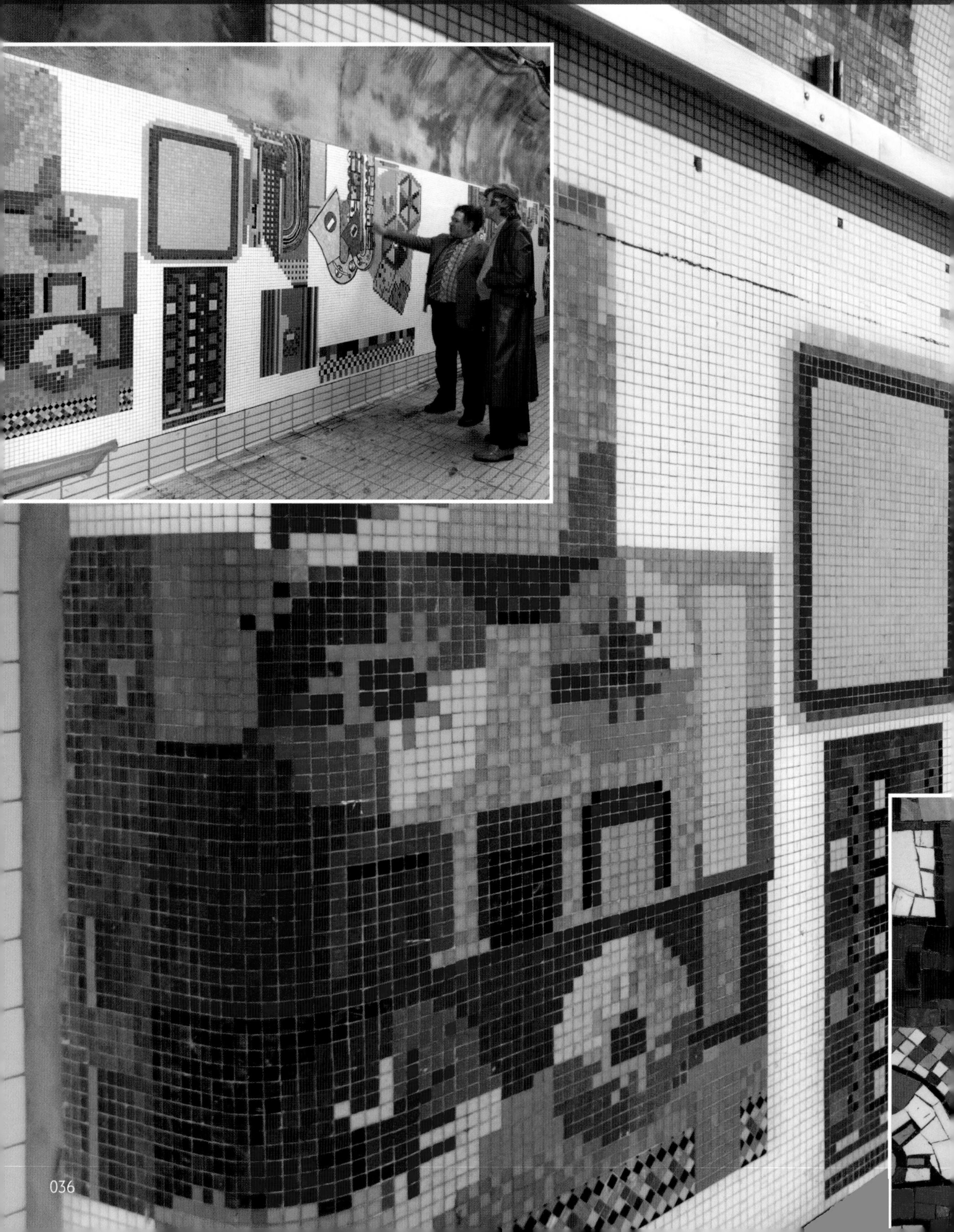

'London Underground invested with great vision and commitment to good design when they commissioned these works from Eduardo Paolozzi.'

CURATOR'S NOTES

During the 1980s, London Transport took on the task of refurbishing many central London Underground stations. Artists and designers were commissioned to give them a fresh look with a local theme.

At Tottenham Court Road, leading British artist Sir Eduardo Paolozzi used mosaics throughout the station. The designs reference the vibrant local music and entertainment culture and the consumer electronics trade set next to industrial images of cogs, pistons and wheels.

Paolozzi's mosaics are one of the most spectacular examples of post-war public art. Design and conservation specialists within London Underground have worked closely with the Paolozzi Foundation and specialist contractors to protect and restore them.

WHERE TO SEE IT

Tottenham Court Road station
By bus: 1, 8, 10, 14, 19, 24, 25, 29, 38, 55, 73, 98, 134, 176, 242, 390
By Tube: Tottenham Court Road

See also CAPTIONS TO IMAGES on pages 218–220

WHAT MAKES IT SPECIAL

'As one ascends through the main entrance of the station, there is a sense of loftiness and inspiration.'

CURATOR'S NOTES

One of the leading principles in the design of the Jubilee Line Extension (JLE) stations was to create a feeling of space. Designed by Foster + Partners, Canary Wharf station certainly achieves this.

The huge semi-elliptical canopy above ground draws daylight deep into the concourse. A total of 20 escalators move passengers through all parts of the station. The palette of concrete, glass and metal used throughout the station achieves an austere and robust aesthetic, notably where concrete tunnel walls are left exposed.

WHERE TO SEE IT

Canary Wharf station, Jubilee line
By bus: 135, 277, D3, D7, D8
By Tube: Canary Wharf
By DLR: Canary Wharf, Heron Quays

↑ Jubilee line

WHAT MAKES IT SPECIAL

'Simply beautiful. Less really is more … [it] set the benchmark in Tube train design for decades.'

CURATOR'S NOTES

In the 1930s London's Underground trains were the most advanced in the world. The 1938 Tube stock represented a ground-breaking design that set the basic style of Tube trains right up to the 1980s. It was unique to London, designed to maximise passenger accommodation by ingeniously locating all the control equipment below the floor. The train fitted in the city's deep tunnels and the car interiors felt comfortable and spacious even in rush hour.

WHERE TO SEE IT

London Transport Museum

The Museum has a 1938 Tube stock car on display, and also occasionally operates heritage outings with its preserved 1938 Tube stock train. For information about excursions please see the London Transport Museum website.

'Although a very recent addition to the TfL family, the Overground stations, trains and branding have become instantly recognisable and loved throughout the areas they serve. It is a great example of what is termed in the design industry as "design thinking" and "service design".'

CURATOR'S NOTES

In November 2007, the London Overground was formally launched as part of the Transport for London network, with its own orange and blue roundel. Stations and trains were refurbished and rebranded, and Oyster card readers installed. In April 2010 the former East London line was added.

Visually, the Overground is associated with the Underground by the roundel and use of the New Johnston typeface. New trains introduced air-conditioning for the first time and featured a newly designed moquette created by textile designers Wallace Sewell, incorporating the orange colour of the network.

In 2016 the orbital network serves 112 stations and is used by over 140 million people annually.

WHERE TO SEE IT

London Overground

'... the JLE is a design icon for two principal reasons. Firstly, the consistent high design quality that runs through the project. Secondly, because it showed that London was once again serious about delivering exemplary transport design to improve people's quality of life.'

CURATOR'S NOTES

Construction of the Jubilee Line Extension (JLE) began in December 1993 and was completed in 1999. At the time, it was the largest public architectural commission in the UK since the Festival of Britain in 1951.

In its architectural vision, as conceived by Roland Paoletti (Project Architect), the JLE saw a return to the high standards of the 1930s. London Transport commissioned some of the world's best architects to deliver the JLE project. Although the stations are all individual, they share the same high quality finishes and use similar materials, notably steel panelling and exposed concrete, also colour – Jubilee line grey – and signage.

WHERE TO SEE IT

Jubilee line (Westminster to Stratford)

See also CAPTIONS TO IMAGES on pages 218–220

WHAT MAKES IT SPECIAL

'… *it brings together London's travel heritage of the 1950s and 60s, and incorporates it into the modern 21st century.*'

CURATOR'S NOTES

Heatherwick Studio collaborated with Transport for London and the manufacturers Wrightbus to produce a new bus for London to replace the much-loved 1950s Routemaster.

The brief for the new bus was that it should work more efficiently and use 40 per cent less fuel than other buses. It was also intended that it would pay homage to the original Routemaster. The new design reintroduced the curves of the Routemaster, which creates an illusion that the bus is smaller in comparison to other modern double-decker buses.

WHERE TO SEE IT

Operates on numerous central London bus routes

'Many a time I have fallen asleep on the seats and have woken with the infamous moquette rash, especially in the early days, when the material was a bit coarser.'

CURATOR'S NOTES

Moquette is a woven woollen fabric that can be made in a range of patterns and colours. Durable, hard-wearing and fireproof, but comfortable to sit on, it is ideal for vehicle upholstery. It was first used as a public transport seating fabric in the 1920s.

From 1937 London Transport commissioned its own designers to produce moquette patterns. The classic designs that followed were used on the Underground and surface transport for many decades. Today, fresh and distinctive moquette patterns continue to be designed for projects, including the New Routemaster and the New Tube for London.

WHERE TO SEE IT

Moquette seating fabric can be seen on every Transport for London bus, Tube, Docklands Light Railway, Overground train and Tramlink.

London Transport Museum

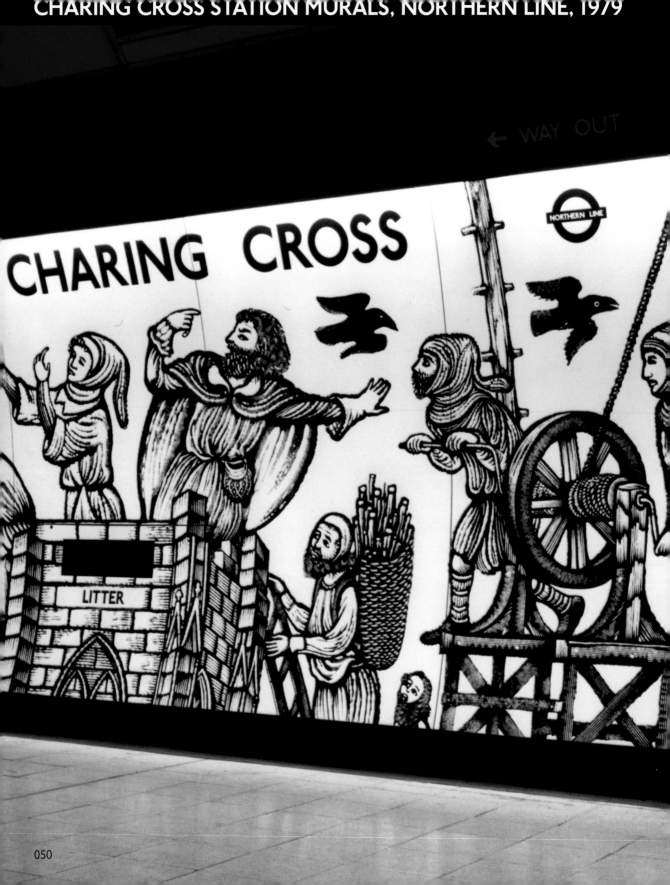

'I love that each Underground station is designed with the history of the station and area in mind.'

CURATOR'S NOTES

For almost 90 years the predominant decoration for Underground platforms was tiling. However, at the end of the 1970s panelling was tried. One of the first panelled stations was Charing Cross, which included black and white murals on the Northern line platform, created by the artist David Gentleman.

The murals depict the construction of the medieval Eleanor Cross in 1291. Gentleman engraved the images on wood blocks that were then photographically enlarged and printed onto melamine sheets.

WHERE TO SEE IT

Charing Cross station
By bus: 3, 6, 9, 11, 12, 13, 15, 23, 24, 29, 53, 87, 88, 91, 139, 159, 176, 453
By Tube: Charing Cross

GO CONTACTLESS
GO ANYWHERE

NEVER TOP UP AGAIN

For more information, visit tfl.gov.uk/contactless

UK issued cards are accepted. For cards issued outside UK, check tfl.gov.uk/contactless-payment-card, before you travel.
Check with your card issuer for any international transaction fees/charges that may apply.

MAYOR OF LONDON

TRANSPORT FOR LONDON
EVERY JOURNEY MATTERS

'This has become a symbol of London transport. The act of "touching in" and "touching out" is synonymous with the city, and it acts almost as a gateway to London.'

CURATOR'S NOTES

In 2003, Transport for London (TfL) introduced the electronic smartcard ticketing system called Oyster; since then over 60 million cards have been issued. In 2014, TfL enabled passengers to pay for journeys by 'touching in' and 'touching out' with a bank card; and more recently, from a phone.

Smartcard and contactless payment has revolutionised the way people travel around the capital. For most people in London in 2016, travel is now cashless. It saves time, allowing 40 people a minute to pass through ticket gates at stations. It also makes boarding a bus three times faster.

WHERE TO SEE IT

On all Transport for London buses and at Tube, DLR and Overground stations

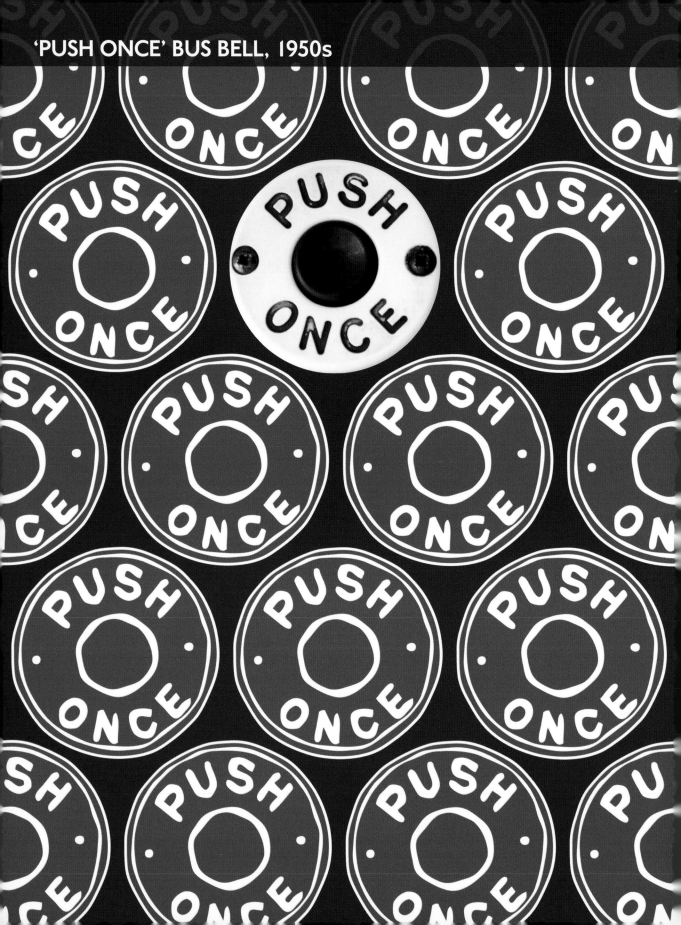

CURATOR'S NOTES

A standardised functional object that
attracts the eye, is pleasing to the touch
and does its job perfectly, this bell was
used on thousands of London buses
over a period of at least 60 years.

Although many variations are used
on every bus in London in 2016, the
traditional and classic 'Push once'
design can be seen on RT and RM type
buses at London Transport Museum.

WHERE TO SEE IT
London Transport Museum

by Julia Black
An adaptation of a William Morris design. He was born and worked for a time in Walthamstow where a museum displays examples of his work.

by Hans Unger
The black horse also appears as a sculpture, by David McFall, on the exterior of the station.

by Edward Bawden
The name is derived from a ferry over the river Lea in earlier times. The word 'hale' is said to be a corruption of 'haul'; or perhaps 'hail'.

by Hans Unger
The seven sisters were seven trees which gave a name to the locality.

by Tom Eckersley
The crossed pistols refer to the duelling that took place here when this was outside the edge of London.

by Edward Bawden
The high bury, manor or castle, was destroyed at the time of the Peasants' Revolt (1381).

by Tom Eckersley
A literal design based on a cross and crowns. The King concerned (if there ever was one) is not identified.

by Tom Eckersley
A reminder of the Doric Arch which stood on the station site.

by Crosby/Fletcher/Forbes
A maze or Warren as a pun on the name. A solution is possible for the traveller with time to spare.

by Hans Unger
A device to incorporate the circle of the circus with the linking of the Bakerloo, Central and Victoria Lines.

by Hans Unger
A bird's eye view of the trees in the park against the green background of the grass.

by Edward Bawden
The great Queen herself, from a silhouette by Benjamin Pearce. A plaque in the ticket hall records the visit of Queen Elizabeth to open the Victoria Line in March 1969.

All these motif designs, specially commissioned for the twelve stations so far open on the Victoria Line, are reproduced in full colour in a folder obtainable price 1/- at any main London Transport Travel Enquiry Office (including those on the Victoria Line at Euston, Oxford Circus and Victoria Stations). Or post free from the Public Relations Officer, 55 Broadway, S.W.1. Copies of this poster cost 12/6

'The platform motifs and murals are a part of what demonstrates London Underground's rich heritage, iconic legacy and aesthetic appeal.'

CURATOR'S NOTES

The Victoria line opened in stages, between 1968 and 1972. On 7 March 1969, Queen Elizabeth travelled on the train, marking the line's official opening. London Transport commissioned the Design Research Unit (DRU) headed by Misha Black to style the line, which had few surface buildings. The DRU incorporated art into the stations above and below ground. To enliven the predominantly grey tiles on the platforms, well-known designers and artists produced individual tile panels to decorate seating niches. The designs were inspired by and related to the station name or local area. For example, Edward Bawden's tiles for Highbury & Islington station feature a local castle destroyed in the 13th century.

All stations still have the motifs. Some have been restored, in other cases (like Green Park) original designs have been reinstated where they had been replaced with different designs.

WHERE TO SEE IT
By Tube: **Victoria line**

'LEGIBLE LONDON' WAYFINDING SYSTEM, 2007

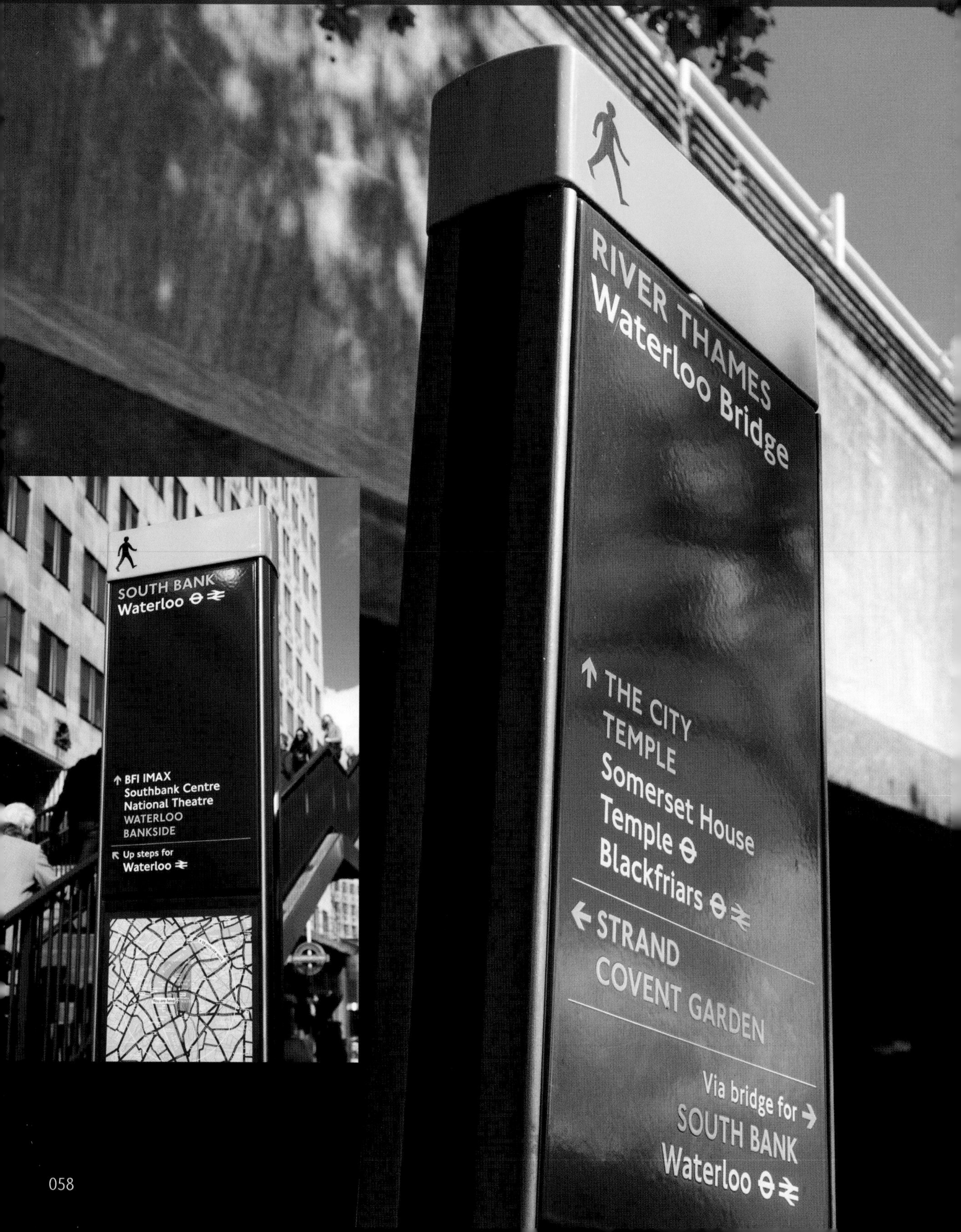

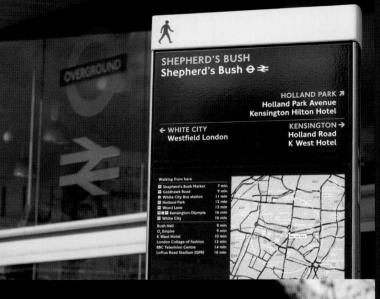

WHAT MAKES IT SPECIAL

'… you can spot them wherever you are in London. I also believe that they are the secret backbone of the London transport network.'

CURATOR'S NOTES

Legible London is an easy-to-use pedestrian signage system designed to help people find their way, and encourage walking in the capital. It presents consistent information in a range of ways, including maps and directional information. The first set of 19 street signs were installed in the Bond Street area of central London in 2007; in 2016 there are over 1,500 maps and signs across the city, at all Tube and mainline rail stations, bus stops and Cycle Hire docking stations. The system was developed by AIG (Applied Information Group, now Applied Wayfinding) and Transport for London, working with London boroughs and business organisations.

WHERE TO SEE IT

Across most of inner London

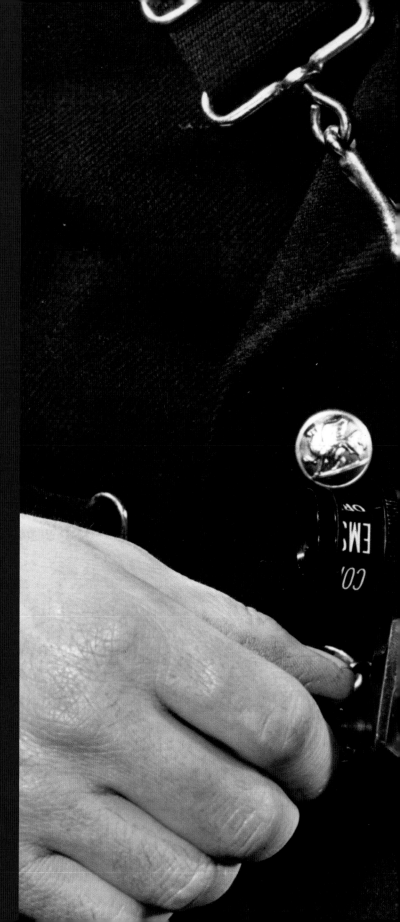

'I love the shiny metal exterior of this ticket machine.'

CURATOR'S NOTES

This ingenious machine was named after its inventor, George Gibson, who was the manager of London Transport's ticket works at Brixton in London. The Gibson could be set to print any combination of ticket code and fare value, allowing a range of different tickets to be printed on a single roll of paper. It quickly replaced the Bell Punch system that had been used in London for 60 years, with its costly, individual pre-printed tickets.

By accurately recording the value and number of tickets issued, the Gibson made fare collection accountable and prevented fraud. At its height, there were some 15,000 Gibson machines in operation, consuming between them about 241,000km (150,000 miles) of paper every year. The last ones were withdrawn in 1993.

WHERE TO SEE IT
London Transport Museum

WHAT MAKES IT SPECIAL

'Still vibrant almost 90 years after it first appeared to brighten London Underground stations, it is easy to imagine how effective it must have been at the dawn of the jazz age.'

CURATOR'S NOTES

In a city still recovering from the First World War, vibrant posters like this one by Horace Taylor splashed colour into 1920s London. The Underground is presented as bright, popular and fashionable. At the time the poster was issued, the three escalators represented modernity. In reality, Bank was the only station boasting a triple escalator.

Horace Taylor's granddaughter once explained that Taylor often liked to paint himself into his posters. In this one he is the bearded gentleman with the top hat on the right.

WHERE TO SEE IT
Museum Depot

BRIGHTEST LONDON

IS BEST REACHED BY

UNDERGROUND

'One of the main memories (yes, really) of using the Tube as a little one on day trips to London is seeing these dangly baubles in the Tube carriages.'

CURATOR'S NOTES

While early Tube trains were rarely overcrowded compared to peak times today, provision has always been made for standing passengers. Simple leather loops or straphangers, running along bars above seats, were used until the 1920s, when loops of harder material were introduced, followed by the simpler bulb-shaped 'hand-grabs' of the late 1930s.

Modern train interiors have been designed to increase capacity by accommodating a higher proportion of standing passengers. Most hand-grabs have been replaced by simpler bars and posts.

WHERE TO SEE IT

London Transport Museum

The Museum has a 1938 Tube stock car on display, and also occasionally operates heritage outings with its preserved 1938 Tube stock train. For information about excursions please see the London Transport Museum website.

B. Dixie. delin.

CURATOR'S NOTES

Construction of the Thames Tunnel between Wapping and Rotherhithe began in 1825. The first underwater tunnel in the world, it was engineered by Marc Brunel and completed by his son, Isambard Kingdom Brunel. The 'great bore', as it came to be called, took nearly 20 years to build, finally opening in 1843.

The tunnel was designed for horse-drawn carriages, but it was never used for this purpose and became an increasingly seedy pedestrian tourist attraction, until it was converted to railway use in the 1860s by the East London Railway. Like so many pioneering projects, the Thames Tunnel was a financial disaster, but an important technological breakthrough. Today it is part of the Overground network.

WHERE TO SEE IT

Rotherhithe station
By bus (to Rotherhithe): 381, C10
By Overground: Wapping, Rotherhithe

See also CAPTIONS TO IMAGES on pages 218–220

'The glass wall at Southwark station is one of my favourite parts of the network. It feels very futuristic but is also somehow comforting.'

CURATOR'S NOTES

Southwark station's magnificent blue curving wall was designed by Alexander Beleschenko and inspired by an 1816 stage set for *The Magic Flute* opera. It was incorporated into the overall design of the station by MacCormac Jamieson Prichard.

As one of the 11 Jubilee Line Extension (JLE) stations, Southwark continued the JLE palette of tough, resilient materials (concrete and steel) but with an enhanced quality seen in the use of textured masonry and enamelled glass.

WHERE TO SEE IT

Southwark station
By bus: 1, 45, 63, 100
By Tube: Jubilee line

'It brightens up your day when you get one of those prime "driver" seats, and I'm sure it's many small and big kids' favourite type of journey. Plus the section near West India Quay is a bit like a rollercoaster.'

CURATOR'S NOTES

The Docklands Light Railway (DLR) opened in 1987 with the aim of revitalising the redeveloped Docklands area by providing good public transport links with the rest of the capital. Since 1987 the network has been extended several times.

DLR trains are automatic and driverless. A passenger service agent is on board every train to provide assistance and answer enquiries.

Originally, the train livery was blue and red with white detailing, designed by a London student and selected via a competition. The DLR also used a new style of lettering called Rockwell on all its signage. The service was graphically integrated with the rest of Transport for London in 2005; roundels were put up and New Johnston typeface used for all signage.

WHERE TO SEE IT

DLR runs a network of services in east and southeast London, included on the Tube map.

WHAT MAKES IT SPECIAL

*'It has been constant all my life …
like a beacon … When I see this
sign it feels like home.'*

CURATOR'S NOTES

Bus stop flags, bearing the famous
roundel logo and displaying bus route
numbers, are an established part of
London's street furniture.

Organised queuing for buses was first
introduced during the First World War. In
the 1920s London's biggest bus operator,
the London General Omnibus Company
(LGOC), began experimenting with the
design of bus stop flags. A standard
enamel sign with a curved top somewhat
following the form of the roundel was
introduced. The new roadside signs were
part of efforts to present a unified design
in the visually busy streetscape.

The bus stop flag has evolved over time,
from the early 1920s through to John
Elson's designs, utilising solar power to
light timetables in the 1990s.

WHERE TO SEE IT

The bus stop flag is on every bus
stop in London.

Museum Depot

See also CAPTIONS TO IMAGES on pages 218–220

BUS STOP

13 WEEKDAY

23 WEEKDAY

113

PLEASE
RUSH HOUR TRAVEL

RESTAURANT

WHAT MAKES IT SPECIAL

'The building is distinctive for its Art Deco style ... [it] was listed as Grade II by English Heritage on 1 September 2014.'

CURATOR'S NOTES

Victoria Coach Station was designed by Wallis, Gilbert and Partners for London Coastal Coaches and opened in 1932. It offered centralised, luxury accommodation, replacing a series of vehicle parks around central London. The building featured Art Deco styling also used by the architects for the Firestone Tyre factory in west London (1928, now demolished). The aesthetic was well suited to the mechanised age of motor travel. The artist, Grafton, designed the poster for London Coastal Coaches in 1932.

London Transport took over the running of Victoria Coach Station in 1988. Managed today by Transport for London, it is the main arrival and departure point in London for coaches travelling throughout the UK and Europe. The station is used by 14 million passengers, with over 240,000 coach departures a year.

WHERE TO SEE IT

Victoria Coach Station, Buckingham Palace Road, SW1
By bus: 11, 44, 170, 211, C1, C10
By Tube: Victoria, then a short walk

See also CAPTIONS TO IMAGES on pages 218–220

VICTORIA
COACH
STATION

LONDON COASTAL COACHES LTD

Facilities from Victoria Coach Station include: Regular Express Services throughout the year, Coach Tours (Britain and the Continent), Day and Half-day Excursions, Continental Coach Connections.

Full details of these facilities and tickets from Travel Agencies

ISSUED BY LONDON COASTAL COACHES LTD, VICTORIA COACH STATION, S.W.1.

GRAFTON

WHAT MAKES IT SPECIAL

'The 'Baby on board!' badges are the single most iconic badge to encourage etiquette on London transport.'

CURATOR'S NOTES

The first badges with the roundel and the words 'Baby on board!' were trialled in 2005, when they were given out at International Women's Day events. Transport for London went on to make the badges available to pregnant women using public transport and they have proved very popular ever since.

Research showed that Londoners were often afraid to offer their seat in case they inadvertently offended women who were not pregnant. Having a Baby on board badge makes it easier for other passengers to identify mothers-to-be who would like to be offered a seat. The badges also empower and encourage pregnant women to ask for a seat when they need it.

WHERE TO SEE IT

Badges are available on request from the Transport for London website.

See also CAPTIONS TO IMAGES on pages 218–220

WHAT MAKES IT SPECIAL

'This made me think that London was the coolest and most exciting city in the entire world, and I should leave Kent immediately and go to art college in Camberwell, which I did.'

CURATOR'S NOTES

In 1986, Henry Fitzhugh, London Transport's Head of Publicity, commissioned artist David Booth to produce an artwork for a poster. Booth created a witty adaptation of Beck's Underground map using tubes of paint. At Pimlico, a paint tube stands in place of the Tate and the whole artwork plays on the idea of travelling by 'Tube'.

Booth's poster has become one of London Underground's most popular publicity posters. It has been reprinted many times and sold all over the world.

WHERE TO SEE IT

London Transport Museum

See also CAPTIONS TO IMAGES on pages 218–220

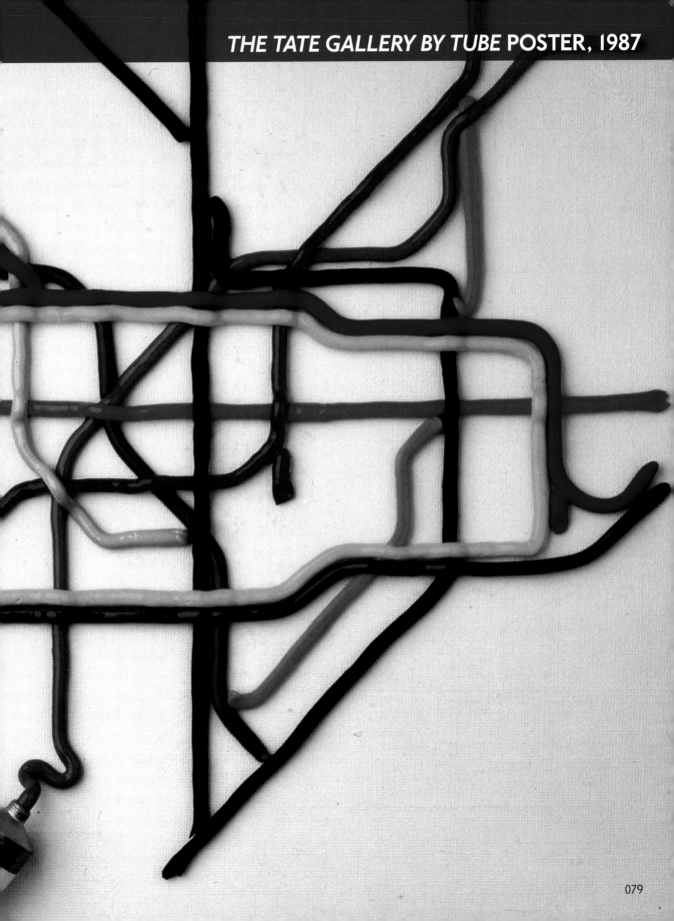

BAKERLOO LINE

PLATFORM 8 SOUTHBOUND ↑

THIS STATION ⬤ BAKER STREET

┃ REGENT'S PARK

◯ OXFORD CIRCUS

◯ PICCADILLY CIRCUS

┃ CHARING CROSS

◯ EMBANKMENT

WATERLOO

'Never sleeping, always serving. A true icon that has stood the test of time.'

CURATOR'S NOTES

The directional signage across all Transport for London networks is connected by a shared visual identity that encompasses the New Johnston typeface, familiar colours, symbols and durable materials. The first standardised sign manual was issued by London Transport in 1938.

Directional signs inform and guide travellers through the network, helping them on their journeys. As designed objects encountered by millions every day, they are the epitome of subtle and effective design.

WHERE TO SEE IT

Across all Transport for London networks

Museum Depot

See also CAPTIONS TO IMAGES on pages 218–220

New Scotl
Bus Sto

£80 penalty fare or prosecution

if you fail to show on demand a ticket, validated smartcard or other travel authority valid for the whole of your journey

Welcome aboard

Buggy users must give priority to wheelchair users

Com
and s

If you have a
London Buse
Website: t
By phone: 0
                      (0.

If you are not s
contact Londor
Website: ww
In writing: Lon

'The on-board "next stop" visual displays and audio announcements make travelling by bus much easier for everyone, especially passengers with visual or hearing impairments.'

CURATOR'S NOTES

The iBus system tracks over 9,000 of London's buses using a combination of advanced GPS based tracking technologies. The system triggers automatic audio announcements and visual displays inside each bus telling passengers where they are on the route. It also provides service control facilities, produces performance statistics and the payments to the bus operating companies. iBus calculates the predicted arrival time for all buses at London's 19,000 stops. Passengers can see how long they have to wait by looking on the web, on the Countdown panels in bus shelters, or by using one of the numerous smartphone apps.

WHERE TO SEE IT

On all London buses, at many bus stops and on smartphones

WHAT MAKES IT SPECIAL

'This is a fantastic design, accommodating all users and recreating an important iconic cultural place for people to enjoy.'

CURATOR'S NOTES

Foster + Partners's redesign of Trafalgar Square was completed in 2003, following consultations with 180 separate institutions and thousands of individuals. The most significant change was the closure of the north side of the square to traffic and the creation of a broad new terrace in front of the National Gallery. This links via a flight of steps into the main body of the square.

The redesign also included a platform lift to the main square, improved paving, lighting and traffic signage.

WHERE TO SEE IT

Trafalgar Square
By bus: 3, 6, 9, 11, 12, 13, 15, 23, 24, 29, 53, 87, 88, 91, 94, 139, 159, 176, 453
By Tube: Charing Cross

See also CAPTIONS TO IMAGES on pages 218–220

'... *probably the first major city-wide brand that defined London as a metropolis as opposed to a collection of boroughs, bringing a single logo that has come to define what it is to be part of London.'*

CURATOR'S NOTES

The 'big U, big D' Underground logo was added to stations on the District Railway and the three new Tube lines owned by the Underground Electric Railways Company of London (UERL) in 1908. The new brand was also added to the first pocket maps of the network issued the same year.

WHERE TO SEE IT

Still *in situ* on the exterior of some stations on the Bakerloo, District, Northern and Piccadilly lines. For example, at Chalk Farm, Covent Garden and Maida Vale stations.

See also CAPTIONS TO IMAGES on pages 218–220

FIRST UNDERGROUND LOGO, 1908

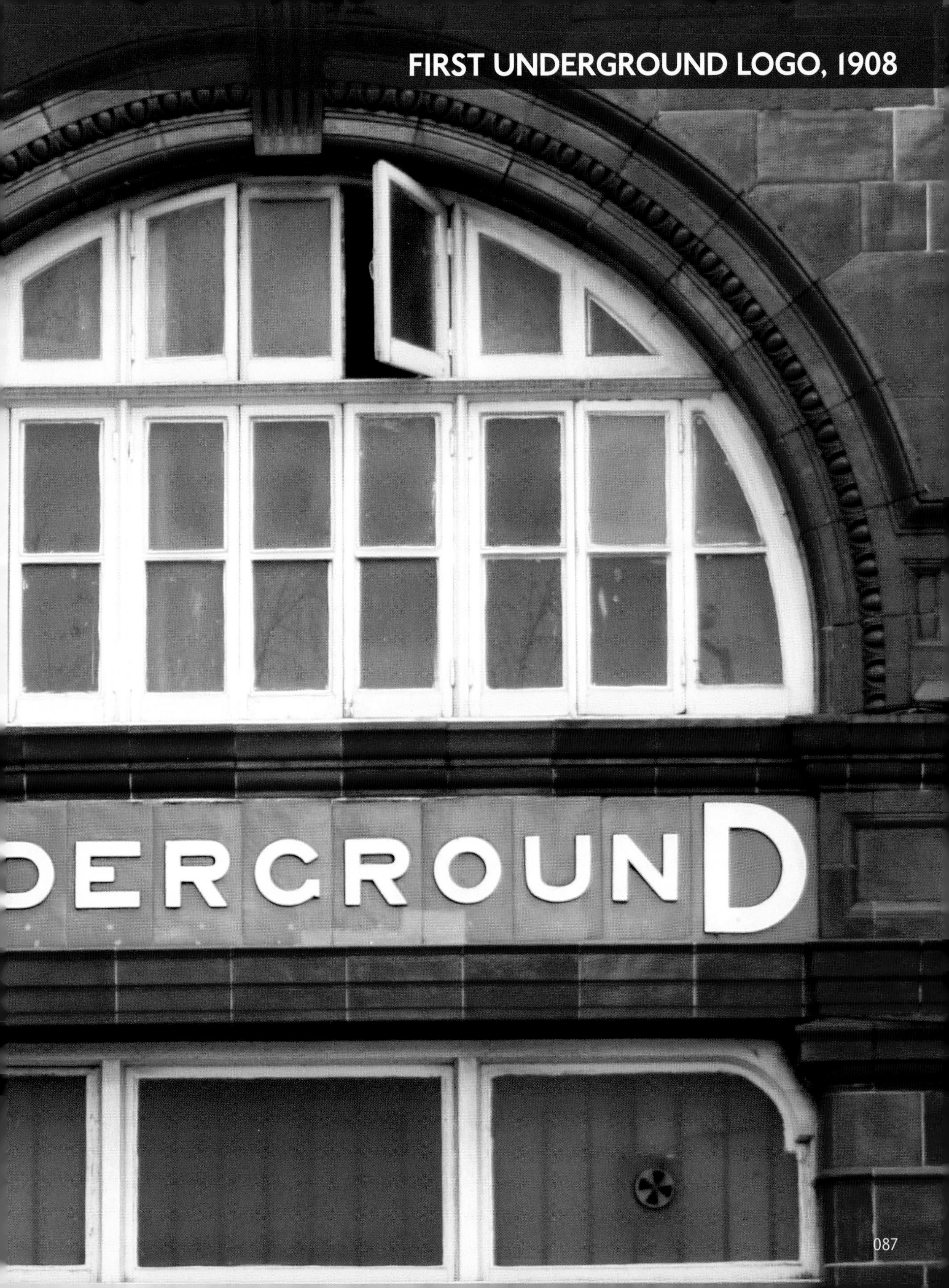

WHAT MAKES IT SPECIAL

'It is most impressive for the way that the two exits on the southern side of Piccadilly so effectively integrate into two very different contexts – the park and the street.'

CURATOR'S NOTES

Green Park station opened in 1933, replacing an earlier station on the site. Extensive modifications have been made since then, most recently in 2011 when the new southern entrance to Green Park station opened. The upgrade included a new canopy and staircase, an attractive ramped entrance with views of the park, and a beautiful artwork, called *Sea Strata* by John Maine RA, commissioned by Art on the Underground. Working with 150-million-year-old Portland stone, Maine created an intricate fossil-clad surface for the station's new Green Park side buildings, and fossil-inspired spiral designs in the paving for the street level access to the Tube.

WHERE TO SEE IT

Green Park station
By bus: 9, 14,19, 22, 38, C2
By Tube: **Green Park**

WHAT MAKES IT SPECIAL

'… the building represented the stature and importance of transport in London at the time.'

CURATOR'S NOTES

Frank Pick selected Charles Holden as architect for the Underground Group's new headquarters, to be constructed over St James's Park station. Holden's ingenious solution for what was an awkward site depended on a cruciform plan, allowing good lighting to all the offices, with minimum impact on surrounding buildings. Opened in 1929, the building was revolutionary, and won the London Architectural Medal. It was also the tallest office building in London at the time.

On the façade Holden included Modernist sculptures by Jacob Epstein, Henry Moore and Eric Gill. Epstein's grouping *Night* (pictured) was dramatic, but the nude figure in *Day* proved controversial and was subsequently altered.

WHERE TO SEE IT

55 Broadway, London SW1H 0BD
As the building is still occupied by Transport for London, public access to the interior is restricted.
By bus: 11, 24, 14, 88, 211 to New Scotland Yard, then short walk
By Tube: St James's Park

See also CAPTIONS TO IMAGES on pages 218–220

WHAT MAKES IT SPECIAL

'[the] Tube map cover series brings art to everyone ... putting art into the hands of millions of people every day.'

CURATOR'S NOTES

Art on the Underground is London Underground's contemporary art programme. Since 2004, Art on the Underground has been commissioning leading artists to create unique artworks for the front cover of the pocket Tube map, with 23 editions to date. In different ways each artwork responds to the map's iconic design and the city it represents.

Top row, left to right

Polka Dots Festival in London, Yayoi Kusama, 2011
Map of London Underground, David Shrigley, 2006
The Hole of London 2014, Rachel Whiteread, 2014
All Time Would be Perpetual Spring,
Imran Qureshi, 2013
Earth, Richard Long, 2009

Bottom row, left to right

Good Times, Eva Rothschild, 2011
Underground Abstract, Cornelia Parker, 2008
The Day Before (You know what they'll call it, they'll call it the Tube), Liam Gillick, 2007
Petrobras [Rio], Sarah Morris, 2012
Global Underground Map, Yinka Shonibare, 2006

WHERE TO SEE IT

The latest pocket Tube maps are available free of charge from every Underground and Overground station.

London Transport Museum
Here you can see a collection of covers.

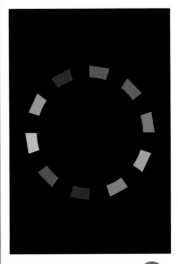

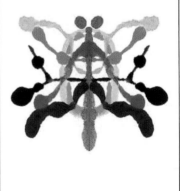

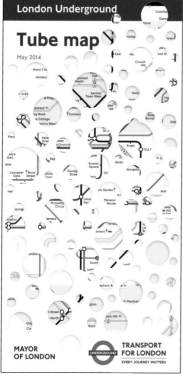

London Underground
Tube map
May 2014

MAYOR OF LONDON · TRANSPORT FOR LONDON · EVERY JOURNEY MATTERS

London Underground
Tube map
December 2013

MAYOR OF LONDON · TRANSPORT FOR LONDON · EVERY JOURNEY MATTERS

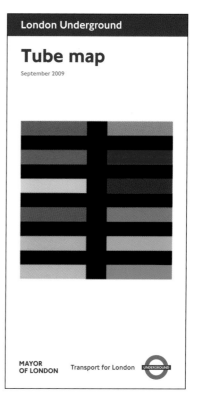

London Underground
Tube map
September 2009

MAYOR OF LONDON · Transport for London

London Underground
Tube map
May 2007

fridayjanu
arythenint
heighteen
sixtythree.

MAYOR OF LONDON · Transport for London

London Underground
Tube map
December 2012

MAYOR OF LONDON · Transport for London · 150

London Underground
Tube map
June 2006

MAYOR OF LONDON · Transport for London

WHAT MAKES IT SPECIAL

'... described at the time as a "Tokyo-style crossing", the distinctive design has come into its own as a London icon, and is regularly seen in both tourist photography and official publications. It also follows the tenets of good design (unique, simple, bold, minimal and replicable).'

CURATOR'S NOTES

Scramble crossings are pedestrian crossings, used in conjunction with traffic signals, where all traffic movement is stopped to allow pedestrians to cross in every direction at the same time. They are widely used in Japan and North America.

The crossing at Oxford Circus in central London was designed by Atkins on behalf of Transport for London, The Crown Estate, Westminster City Council and the New West End Company, and installed during 2009.

WHERE TO SEE IT

Oxford Circus
By bus: 3, 6, 7, 10, 12, 13, 23, 25, 55, 73, 88, 94, 98, 137, 139, 189, 390, 453, C2
By Tube: Oxford Circus

OXFORD CIRCUS 'SCRAMBLE' CROSSING, 2009

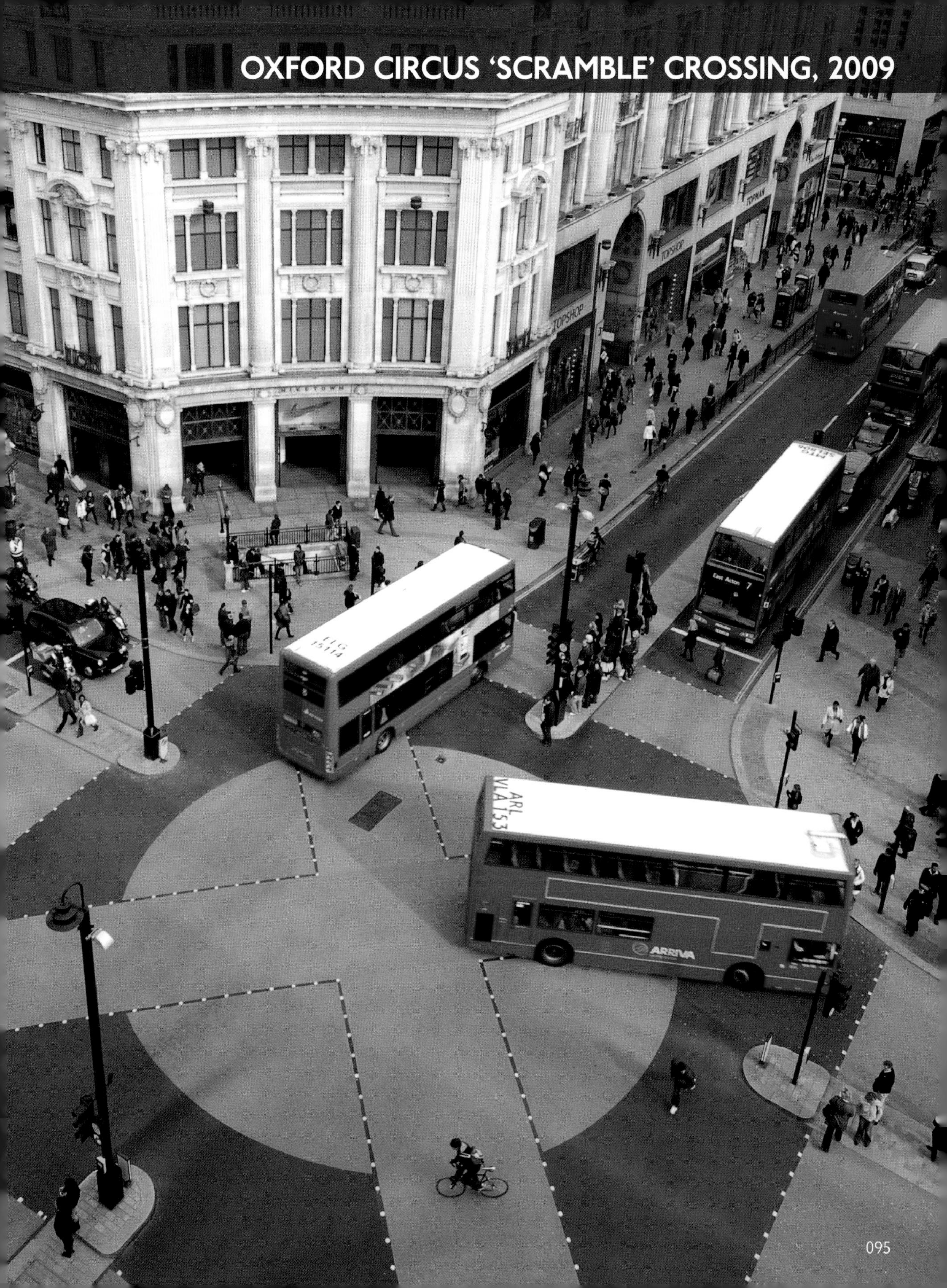

'I've travelled to these stations many times just to marvel at the architecture … Arnos Grove, in particular, is a classic. The large windows bring natural light into the station, with the passimeter – still in existence! – standing as a sentinel to customers in need of assistance.'

CURATOR'S NOTES

The Piccadilly Line Extension stations built between 1931 and 1933 are generally acknowledged as the architect Charles Holden's best work. The first five new stations north of Finsbury Park, including Arnos Grove, opened in September 1932. Holden's restrained Modernism, characterised by attention to detail and a commitment to total design, combined a unified look with subtle variety.

WHERE TO SEE IT

Piccadilly line (Manor House to Arnos Grove)
By bus: Numerous bus routes
By Tube: Piccadilly line

DIRECT FROM PICCADILLY

Manor House   16
Turnpike Lane   19
Wood Green   2
Bounds Green   23
Arnos Grove   25

See also CAPTIONS TO IMAGES on pages 218–220

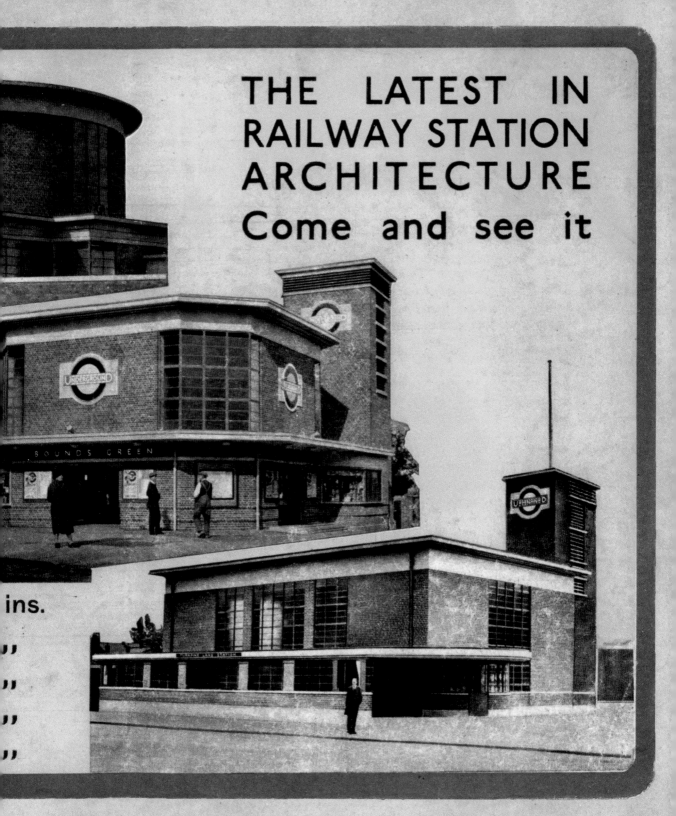

THE LATEST IN RAILWAY STATION ARCHITECTURE
Come and see it

ins.

"

"

"

"

'... *when the new trains were introduced at the opening of the Victoria line, they were seen as the advent of a modern age. The Victoria line cut travel time across central London, and was the first London Underground line to use automatic train operation – an amazing feat for a train constructed in the 1960s.*'

CURATOR'S NOTES

The Victoria line was the most advanced underground railway in the world when it opened in 1968, with computer-controlled trains and automatic ticket barriers. The unpainted silver finish and wrap-around windscreens of the trains gave London's new Tube a fashionable space-age look that was part of the Design Research Unit's visual concept for the whole line.

WHERE TO SEE IT

One car of 1967 Tube stock is preserved at the Museum Depot.

See also CAPTIONS TO IMAGES on pages 218–220

'Rather lovely oddities – and it is particularly impressive that so much thought and care had been given to the design and manufacture of a very mundane and functional item.'

CURATOR'S NOTES

During the 1930s, decorative metalwork was incorporated into the design of the Piccadilly Line Extension to Cockfosters. Manor House, as well as Turnpike Lane and Wood Green, had ornate grilles installed over the ventilation ducts placed along the platform walls. The grilles were designed by Harold Stabler and unique to each station.

WHERE TO SEE IT

Manor House station
By bus: 29, 141, 253, 254, 259, 279, 341
By Tube: **Manor House**

See also CAPTIONS TO IMAGES on pages 218–220

WHAT MAKES IT SPECIAL

'I love some of the old tiles at stations such as Edgware Road and Mornington Crescent. Very classic-looking, and they respect the Tube's illustrious history.'

CURATOR'S NOTES

From at least the 1860s onwards, glazed tiles have been chosen for Underground station interiors because they are durable and easy to clean. Leslie Green's 1906–7 Tube stations feature plain white and green tiles and mouldings at street level. At platform level the station name and instructions such as 'Way Out' and 'To Trains' are also rendered in tile, alongside individual colour schemes in repeating geometric patterns right along the platform.

At the surviving Leslie Green stations, the exterior, interior and platforms remain largely as designed, but with some sections refurbished.

WHERE TO SEE IT

There are still many stations designed by Leslie Green in use on the Tube network. Good examples in daily use are Mornington Crescent and Covent Garden.

See also CAPTIONS TO IMAGES on pages 218–220

'The arched roof makes it appear as if the whole station is about to sail away through the waters of Canary Wharf.'

CURATOR'S NOTES

Canary Wharf will be one of the largest stations on the new Crossrail line, linking east and southeast London with west London, Heathrow Airport and Berkshire.

Foster + Partners were the principal architects for the seven-storey building, which is crowned with a roof of special plastic, aluminium and timber.

Beneath the roof is an ornamental garden, and below that a shopping centre, both of which opened in May 2015. The station platforms open for business when Crossrail commences operations in late 2018.

WHERE TO SEE IT

The roof terrace at Canary Wharf Crossrail station is open to the public. The main station is scheduled to open in December 2018.
By bus: 135, 277, D3, D7, D8
By Tube: Canary Wharf
By DLR: Canary Wharf, West India Quay

See also CAPTIONS TO IMAGES on pages 218–220

WHAT MAKES IT SPECIAL

'Covent Garden station has always been the symbol of London to me, and travelling through it makes me feel like I'm at the centre of the universe. As with all of Leslie Green's stations, it doesn't look dated, just classic.'

CURATOR'S NOTES

The station was designed by Leslie Green and opened in 1907. It retains much of its original character, while at the same time it has been upgraded in 2015 with new high-speed lifts.

It primarily served the large fruit, flower and vegetable markets in Covent Garden. With the closure of the markets in the 1970s, the area slowly transformed into a busy and attractive shopping area, popular with tourists. London Transport Museum now occupies the former Flower Market building in the nearby Piazza.

WHERE TO SEE IT

Covent Garden station
By bus: 1, 4, 6, 9, 11, 13, 15, 23, 26, 59, 68, 76, 87, 91, 139, 168, 171, 172, 176, 188, 243, 341, 521, RV1
By Tube: Covent Garden

See also CAPTIONS TO IMAGES on pages 218–220

11 ST

'Pedestrian countdown signals that tell people how much longer they have to cross the road have become a widely used and dependable tool.'

CURATOR'S NOTES

In 2008, Transport for London (TfL) proposed the adoption of Pedestrian Countdown at Traffic Signals (PCaTS) in London, to improve pedestrian crossings. The signals allow people, particularly those with accessibility issues, to cross in the knowledge that they have enough time. This helps to cut down the number of road accidents.

TfL developed the system, working with the Department for Transport and the Highways Agency. Twenty-nine combinations of red and green men and countdown panel configurations were considered. After studies of similar systems in Dublin, New York, San Francisco and Auckland, a London version was tested on eight crossings in 2011. Countdown timers have now been installed at 400 sites across the capital, and are an increasingly common sight throughout London as pedestrian crossings at busy road crossings are remodelled or modernised.

WHERE TO SEE IT
Pedestrian crossings all over London

WHAT MAKES IT SPECIAL

'By proudly declaring the bus's route, the blinds have helped countless millions of people on their journey in a manner and style that is as simple as it is informative.'

CURATOR'S NOTES

Destinations and stopping points have been displayed on buses since 1829, when bus services first began. But as services developed and became more complex, roller blinds were adopted in the 1920s. In the 1930s they were silk-screen printed onto paper strips that were then pasted onto rolls of linen up to 10m (30ft) long.

Modern blinds are still silk-screen printed, but applied straight onto rolls of man-made fabric, which can be much longer.

WHERE TO SEE IT

Bus blinds can be seen on every London bus.

See also CAPTIONS TO IMAGES on pages 218–220

'It has helped keep London's buses moving since 1968.'

CURATOR'S NOTES

Bus-only lanes were introduced in London in 1968 to keep buses moving and reduce the delays caused by traffic congestion. The number of bus lanes has risen considerably since then, and now bus lanes are not just for buses – taxis, motorcyclists and cyclists can use many of them too.

WHERE TO SEE IT

All over the Transport for London road network

See also CAPTIONS TO IMAGES on pages 218–220

EAST FINCHLEY *ARCHER*, 1940

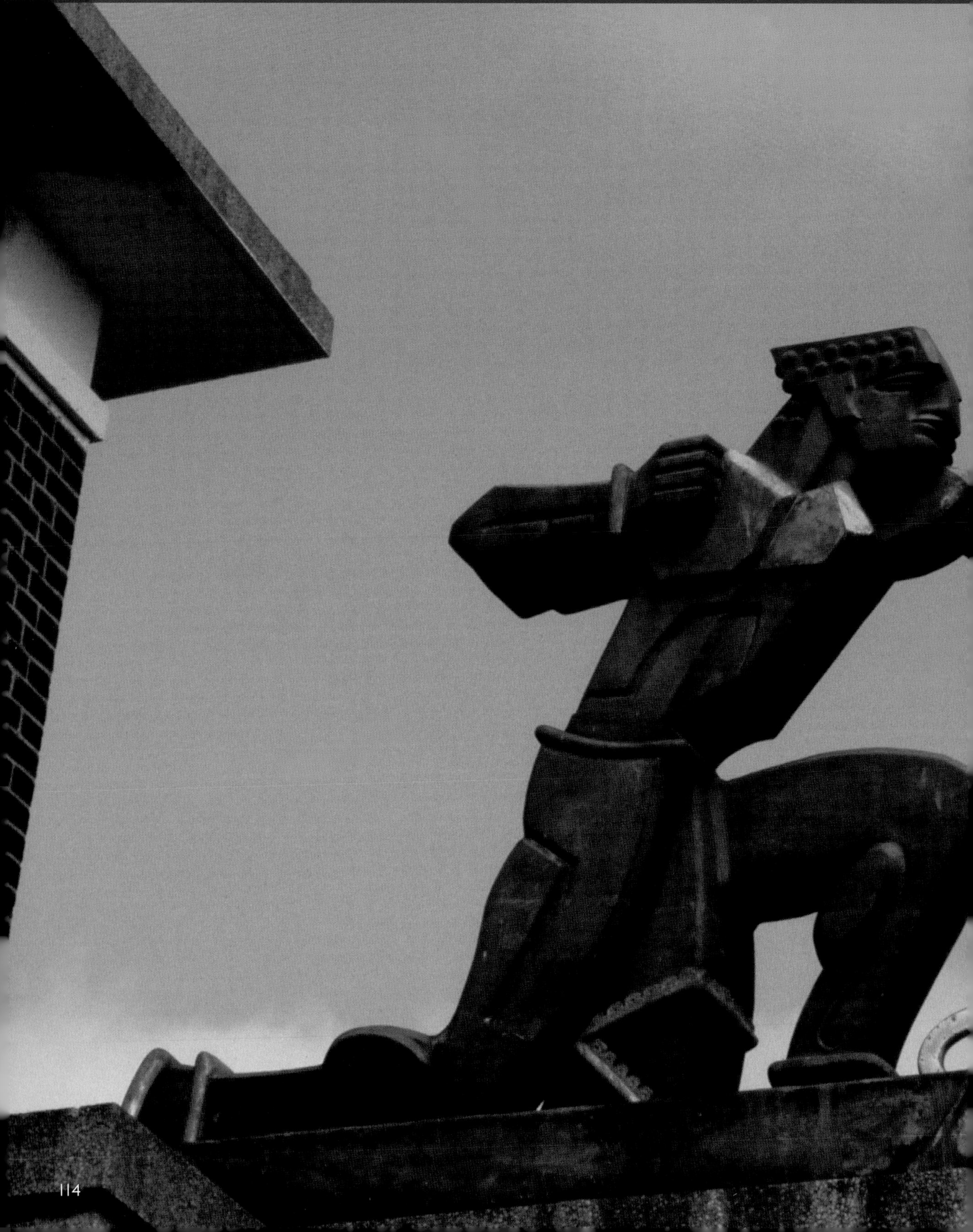

WHAT MAKES IT SPECIAL

'I commute from East Finchley and always position myself under The Archer. *He is an ancient symbol representing the royal forest of Enfield, a local paper is named after him, and rumour has it that he has shot his arrow all the way to Morden. I love the Art Deco style, and I always point him out to people on my local history walks.'*

CURATOR'S NOTES

Eric Aumonier, who created *The Archer*, joined the family firm of architectural sculptors after finishing his studies at the Slade School of Art in the early 1920s. The commission for East Finchley station was one of three from London Transport, including representations of the South Wind on the exterior of 55 Broadway, and a pie with a knife and fork over the entrance to the canteen at the Underground's Acton engineering works. A fourth commission at Archway station was interrupted by the outbreak of the Second World War, but luckily, East Finchley (and with it *The Archer*) was completed in 1940.

WHERE TO SEE IT

East Finchley station
By bus: 102, 143, 234, 263, H3
By Tube: East Finchley

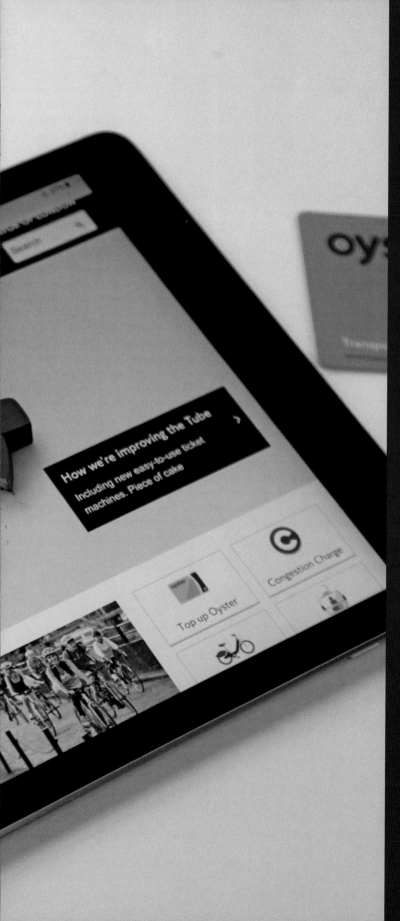

'The TfL Journey Planner liberates Londoners from timetables and maps, providing a bespoke personal guide to real travel times and modal options wherever you are in the city.'

CURATOR'S NOTES

The Journey Planner in use today evolved from the first computerised database of travel routes across London, initially used only by London Transport staff operating the travel information service. They relayed travel advice and instructions to members of the public on the telephone.

In July 2002 the online Journey Planner was launched by Transport for London. By the end of the year it was already being consulted by over a million users a month. A version for smartphones and tablets was launched in 2010.

The user interface is intuitive and civilises the complexity and richness of London.

WHERE TO SEE IT

Transport for London website

'This incredible Surrealist image places the symbol of the Underground on a par with Saturn.'

CURATOR'S NOTES

This image is one of the most familiar in the London Transport Museum's collection. Two versions of the poster were printed using the same image, but with different wording underneath. Designed to be displayed together as in the photograph, the one on the left says 'London Transport', the one on the right, 'Keeps London Going'.

Produced by the famous Surrealist and Dadaist Man Ray during a brief residence in London, the posters feature the iconic roundel in the form of a planet.

The image is a photogram, a picture produced with photographic materials, such as light-sensitive paper, but without a camera. Man Ray experimented with this 19th century technique by varying the exposure times given to different objects within a single photogram, and by moving the objects during light exposure. He then renamed the process a rayograph, after himself.

WHERE TO SEE IT
Museum Depot

See also CAPTIONS TO IMAGES on pages 218–220

-KEEPS LONDON GOING

Night Tube
Operates on Friday and Saturday nights

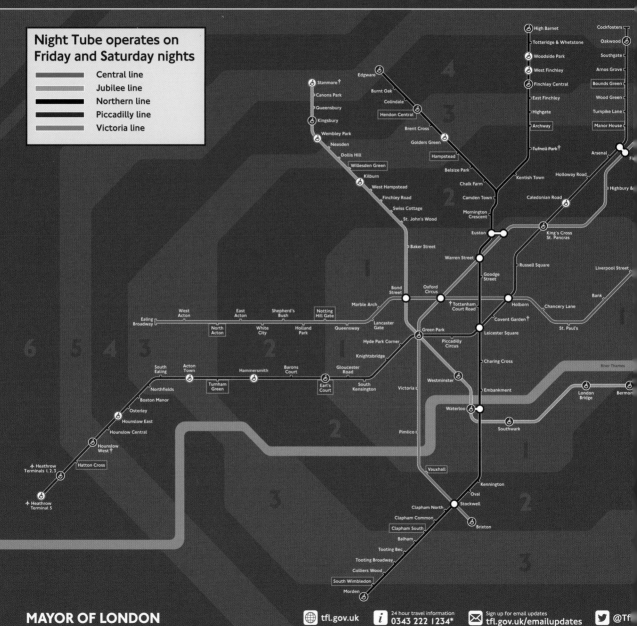

Night Tube operates on Friday and Saturday nights

- Central line
- Jubilee line
- Northern line
- Piccadilly line
- Victoria line

tfl.gov.uk

24 hour travel information
0343 222 1234*

Sign up for email updates
tfl.gov.uk/emailupdates

@Tf

*Service and network charges may apply. See tfl.gov.uk/terms for details.

Night Tube Service

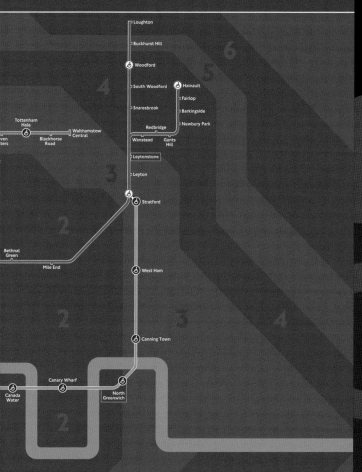

Loughton
Buckhurst Hill
Woodford
South Woodford
Hainault
Fairlop
Snaresbrook
Barkingside
Redbridge
Newbury Park
Tottenham Hale
Wanstead
Gants Hill
Walthamstow Central
Blackhorse Road
Leytonstone
Leyton
Stratford
Bethnal Green
Mile End
West Ham
Canning Town
Canary Wharf
North Greenwich
Canada Water

4 5 6 3 2 2 3 4 2

Manor House Station in both fare zones

O Interchange stations

Step-free access from street to train

Step-free access from street to platform

✈ Airport

† **Covent Garden** Exit only until early November 2015. Also, on Saturdays and Sundays, westbound trains will not stop. Please use Leicester Square instead.

Hounslow West Step-free access for manual wheelchairs only.

Stanmore Step-free access via a steep ramp.

Tottenham Court Road Central line trains will not stop at this station until early December 2015.

Tufnell Park Temporary station closure until mid-March 2016.

Alerts

UNDERGROUND

TRANSPORT FOR LONDON

EVERY JOURNEY MATTERS

---

only apply to the daytime service, the Night Tube map delivers information that is grounded in clarity, but also resonates with the spirit of night services.'

CURATOR'S NOTES

The launch of an all-night Friday and Saturday Tube service on five lines is expected in 2016. Designing a night Tube map that clearly but legibly differentiates from the more complex day map was challenging. Both maps will be displayed together on station platforms, so great care has been taken to keep the scale and design values in sympathy, but the background colours and detailing of the new map as different as possible.

Note the appearance of a new night owl symbol, inspired by the 'night owl' logo first applied to London Transport marketing material in 1982. The new version also references elements of New Johnston typography.

WHERE TO SEE IT

Transport for London website

WHAT MAKES IT SPECIAL

'Underground in Bloom makes me SO HAPPY! It's about station staff taking the time to make their stations a little bit more beautiful, and it's something the customers love. Many of the staff build on displays year after year, which means they can be quite elaborate. Often people in the community participate by donating supplies to keep the gardens going.'

CURATOR'S NOTES

Great pride has always been taken in the appearance of London Underground stations, as well as the service provided. On the open sections of the Underground, station garden competitions started before the First World War and have continued in one form or another since then. Garden displays moved up in the public consciousness in 2002, when the competition was rebranded Underground in Bloom. The number of stations competing across the network has risen steadily in the past decade, and there are now around 70 entrants.

WHERE TO SEE IT

Underground stations

See also CAPTIONS TO IMAGES on pages 218—220

WHAT MAKES IT SPECIAL

'The wonderful roundel clock at Gants Hill Underground station makes checking the time a pleasurable event. It would be great if these were rolled out on the whole system.'

CURATOR'S NOTES

In the 1940s several Underground stations opened on the eastern extension of the Central line from Liverpool Street. Four of them (Bethnal Green, Gants Hill, Redbridge and Wanstead) featured distinctive roundel clocks at platform level, made by the Magneta Time Company Ltd.

On the clock face at Gants Hill there are 13 of the famous roundel logos. The hours are marked by 12 roundels and the final one forms the hour hand itself. Clocks with slightly different styling on the casing are also still in place at Bethnal Green, Redbridge and Wanstead stations.

WHERE TO SEE IT

Gants Hill station
By bus: 66, 123, 128, 150, 167, 179, 296, 396, 462
By Tube: Gants Hill

BUS SPIDER MAP, 2002

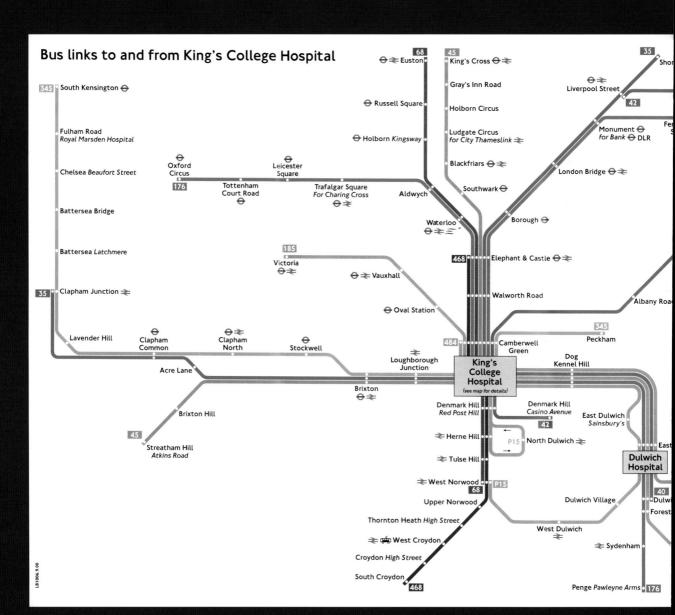

Bus links to and from King's College Hospital

CURATOR'S NOTES

A spider map is a schematic diagram of bus services specific to a local area. They have been used by Transport for London since 2002. The maps are displayed at bus stops around the capital, conveying bus route information in a diagrammatic style similar to that of Henry Beck's Underground map. Routes are numbered on different coloured lines, angled to show some association with geography. Bus stops are indicated with letters on red graphic markers.

The bus maps were designed for Transport for London by the T-Kartor Group, a cartographic design company.

WHERE TO SEE IT
Bus stops across London

40
Aldgate ⊖

Tower of London
for Tower Hill ⊖
and Tower Gateway DLR

Tower Bridge Road

ayers Arms

Bus route	towards	Bus stops	Average route frequency in minutes*
35	Clapham Junction	H6	10
	Shoreditch	H7	10
40	Dulwich	H3	15
	Aldgate	H5	15
42	Denmark Hill	H4	12-15
	Liverpool Street	H1, H5	12-15
45	Streatham Hill	H6	12
	King's Cross Station	H7	12
68	Euston Station	H1, H5	10
	West Norwood	H4	10
176	Penge	H3	10-12
	Oxford Circus	H5	10-12
185	Lewisham	H3	10-12
	Victoria Station	H5	10-12
345	South Kensington	H6	8
	Peckham	H7	8
468	Elephant & Castle	H1, H5	8
	South Croydon	H4	8
484	Lewisham	H3	10
	Camberwell Green	H5	10
P15	West Norwood	H1	30 (Sat daytime)
	North Dulwich	H2	30 (Sat daytime)

*unless otherwise indicated applies to Monday to Saturday midday. Buses may run more frequently during peak hours and less often at other times.

For location of bus stops see map on lower right.

Night buses

N35	Clapham Junction	H6	60
	Tottenham Court Road	H7	60
N68	Old Coulsdon	H4	30
	Tottenham Court Road	H1, H5	30
N176	Penge	H3	30
	Oxford Circus	H5	30

⊖	Tube interchange
≷	National Rail interchange
≷'	Eurostar interchange
DLR	Docklands Light Railway interchange
🚋	Tramlink interchange

Map showing location of bus stops

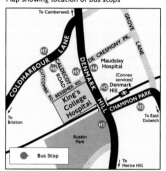

th ≷

cham Rye   Brockley
ry Road   Frendsbury Road

Nunhead
Inverton Road

ary

Telegraph Hill

Brockley ≷
Brockley Cross

Hilly Fields

Ladywell ≷

d ≷

484

185 Lewisham
     ≷ DLR

Lewisham
Hospital

WHAT MAKES IT SPECIAL

'... it is a wonderful design, the lines of the structure are beautiful and striking ... the epitome of modern and practical design.'

CURATOR'S NOTES

Newbury Park bus station was designed by the architect Oliver Hill as one of his last commissions before retirement. Known as a designer of traditional country houses earlier in his career, he was converted to Modernism in the 1930s. His subsequent work typically employed dramatic curving lines, well represented in the Newbury Park design, which won a Festival of Britain Architectural Award in 1951, and is now a Grade II listed building.

WHERE TO SEE IT

Newbury Park bus station
By bus: 66, 296, 396
By Tube: Newbury Park

See also CAPTIONS TO IMAGES on pages 218–220

WHAT MAKES IT SPECIAL

'The double helix towers supporting the Emirates Air Line. I think the structure and design is particularly striking against the background of Canary Wharf.'

CURATOR'S NOTES

The Emirates Air Line cable car opened on Thursday 28 June 2012. It crosses the Thames from Greenwich Peninsula to Royal Docks and provides an interchange with the Jubilee line and Docklands Light Railway. With a journey time of around 10 minutes each way, passengers enjoy spectacular views of London. The cable car can carry up to 2,500 people an hour in each direction and at night the extended journey time offers a unique view across the capital.

WHERE TO SEE IT

North Greenwich
By bus: 108, 129, 132, 161, 188, 422, 472, 486
By Tube: North Greenwich

Royal Victoria
By bus: 147, 241, 474, then a short walk
By DLR: Royal Victoria

WHAT MAKES IT SPECIAL

'One of Britain's best-known designers, David Mellor, had a major impact on surface transport infrastructure, including bus shelters and the traffic signals system.'

CURATOR'S NOTES

David Mellor was an industrial designer who combined the skills of a craftsman and artist with those of a commercial entrepreneur. Best known for his classic stainless-steel cutlery designs, he was also committed to improving the everyday urban environment, including street lighting, bollards, litter bins and, most ubiquitously, the traffic light or 'signal head' that he redesigned in the late 1960s. Although utilitarian, it was designed with a clean simplicity to fit into the urban landscape. Later models built on a modular format allowed a range of traffic signal head configurations to be created, and easily replaced at low cost.

WHERE TO SEE IT

Traffic signals are everywhere on London's streets

WHAT MAKES IT SPECIAL

'Bar a few minor tweaks, the current uniform has been in use for more than 10 years ... The cuts have been refreshed and the fabrics sympathetically reworked for a contemporary look that still reflects the organisation's rich 150-year history.'

CURATOR'S NOTES

Staff working on London's transport network have always been identified by a uniform. It not only represents the organisation, but provides reassurance for the public of a safe and comfortable journey.

In 2015 Transport for London launched a distinctive new uniform for Underground and Overground station staff. Designed by HemingwayDesign, the modern uniforms prominently feature the roundel logo on pockets, jacket cuffs, zip pulls and embroidered on the back of garments. The new uniform was developed with staff input, and reflects London's transport heritage and diversity.

WHERE TO SEE IT

Underground stations on the Tube network

WHAT MAKES IT SPECIAL

'It is one of the first things I can remember that made me think about how things were designed and functioned. It is only a small thing, but a lot of care and attention was spent to ensure that it functioned well, was good to use and would last for the lifetime of the bus.'

CURATOR'S NOTES

Like so many aspects of London Transport vehicle design, the 1950s window winding handle and mechanism on the Routemaster were perfected over several generations of vehicle by the design teams at London Transport's Chiswick Works, getting better and better with each iteration. The winder on the windows of the RF type (1950) and RT type (1939) are very similar and operate with the same mechanism.

WHERE TO SEE IT

Classic heritage Routemaster buses are in service on route 15, between Trafalgar Square and Tower Hill.

London Transport Museum

WHAT MAKES IT SPECIAL

'Piccadilly Circus concourse is filled with hidden design features that go unnoticed by so many ... the materials used in the construction of Piccadilly Circus are both rich and durable, creating a sense of "destination" in the station itself.'

CURATOR'S NOTES

Piccadilly Circus opened in 1906 and it has always been one of the busier Tube stations. By the 1920s, the station was struggling with the traffic passing through, and it was extensively rebuilt with escalators and a new booking hall. Opened in 1928, the redesigned station was by architect Charles Holden, who created an attractive circular hall that welcomed passengers.

Using travertine marble cladding, bronze fittings, glass showcases and roof support columns with hanging lamps, its appearance was similar to an elegant shop, not dissimilar to the establishments found above ground on Regent Street.

WHERE TO SEE IT

Piccadilly Circus station
By bus: 3, 6, 12, 13, 14, 19, 22, 23, 38, 88, 94, 139, 159, 453
By Tube: Piccadilly Circus

See also CAPTIONS TO IMAGES on pages 218–220

'... *it changes the way customers can travel around the city in an eco-friendly and healthy way, and is one of the more recent iconic symbols of London, recognised internationally.*'

CURATOR'S NOTES

The Cycle Hire scheme was introduced in May 2010, initially implemented in 400 locations, with 6,000 bikes. Today there are more than 11,500 bikes and over 760 docking stations covering over 100sq km (36sq miles), with further planned expansion and intensification across the capital. The scheme is sponsored (by Santander in 2016) and was modelled on the Vélib public cycling network in Paris.

More than 47 million journeys have been made on Cycle Hire bikes since the scheme was launched.

WHERE TO SEE IT

Cycle Hire bikes and their docking stations can be found all over central London, and in east and west parts of the capital.

WHAT MAKES IT SPECIAL

'The Earl's Court destination indicators are a delight to behold ... whilst they don't tell you how many minutes to the next train, they tell you the platform, which is what you really need.'

CURATOR'S NOTES

It is Transport for London policy to retain original features that can still be used in their original positions at Underground stations. At Earl's Court station the modern dot matrix destination indicators are supplemented in fine style by the illuminated 'train describer' display board, which has been in use since 1911.

WHERE TO SEE IT

Earl's Court station
(District line platforms)
By bus: 74, 328, C1, C3
By Tube: Earl's Court

See also CAPTIONS TO IMAGES on pages 218–220

WHAT MAKES IT SPECIAL

'*… it has opened a world of exciting apps which help me navigate the city in the most efficient way, and the forward-looking philosophy of transparency invites collaboration, to make London a better city.*'

CURATOR'S NOTES

Open data is data that is made freely available, to be used and republished by anyone without restrictions from copyright or other controls. In 2014, Transport for London began to release live transport information into the public domain. This was done to encourage the growth of digital transport products, which Londoners can use to help them on their journeys. The belief is that the more resources that work on this, the better the overall service. Around 6,000 developers have registered to use the live data feeds. This has led to the production of hundreds of apps reaching millions of passengers.

WHERE TO SEE IT

Smartphone travel apps

'In keeping with the axiom "Good design is invisible", Schleger's bus sign appears to be an effortless reimagining of the London Transport brand.'

CURATOR'S NOTES

In 1935, graphic designer Hans Schleger (also known as Zero) was commissioned to redesign the signs used to indicate bus, coach and tram stopping places. His simplified bullseye consisted of a plain bar and circle in silhouette form. Schleger's stop flags were introduced throughout London, providing the basis for bus stop flags today.

WHERE TO SEE IT
London Transport Museum

HANS SCHLEGER BUS STOP FLAG, 19

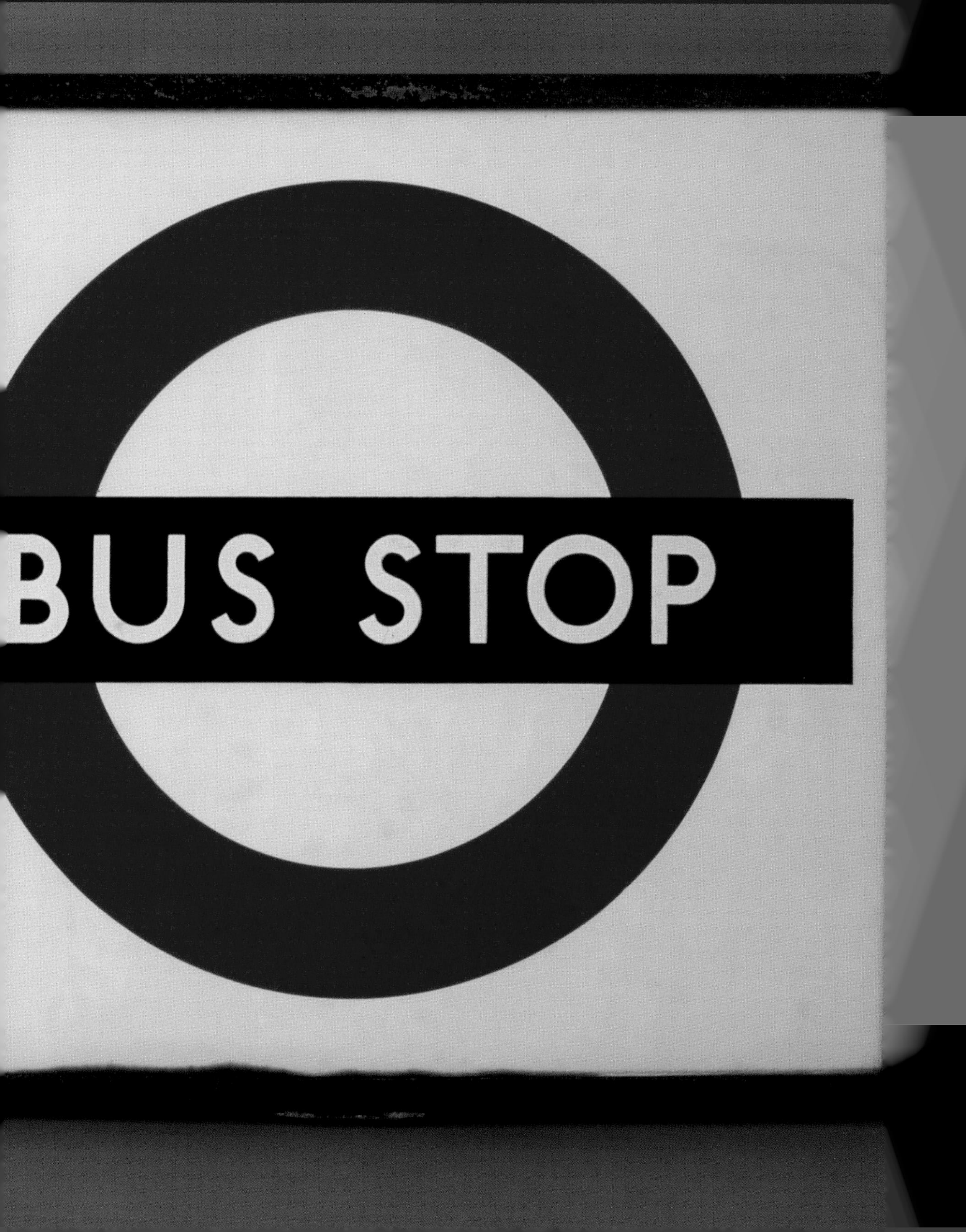

WHAT MAKES IT SPECIAL

'This image sums up for me the best of London Transport as created by Frank Pick. The gold Johnston Sans lettering, edged in black and underlined, combined with the familiar red bus livery, conveys a confident message of quality, unity and dependability.'

CURATOR'S NOTES

With the creation of a single transport authority for London in 1933, gold waterslide transfer lettering was applied to all London Transport buses from 1934 to the late 1960s, surviving on some types of bus until the early 1980s. All new single deck buses introduced from 1968, and new double deck buses from 1970, had either plain Johnston lettering or roundels of various types.

The Johnston version, underlined and with larger letters at the beginning and end, followed the form of the GeneraL fleet name used on buses before the formation of London Transport. That design in turn had followed the form of the 1908 UndergrounD brand.

WHERE TO SEE IT

Classic heritage Routemaster buses are in service on route 15, between Trafalgar Square and Tower Hill.

London Transport Museum
Museum Depot

See also CAPTIONS TO IMAGES on pages 218–220

TRANSPORT

LONDON TRANS

WHAT MAKES IT SPECIAL

'In July 2014 it opened to the public as part of the Year of the Bus open days, and it was inspiring to see so many people amazed by this design icon.'

CURATOR'S NOTES

One of London Transport's most celebrated and radical designs is Stockwell bus garage. Designed by Adie, Button & Partners, it opened in 1952 to replace Norwood tram depot. At the time the arched reinforced concrete roof was the widest unsupported span in Europe.

It is a dramatic piece of architecture, capable of housing 200 buses. It also housed everything the vehicles and drivers required on site, from facilities for inspections, repairs and fuelling to a canteen and staffroom.

It has remained largely unchanged and is now a Grade II* listed building, still operational and fulfilling the same function as when it opened.

WHERE TO SEE IT

Stockwell is an operational bus garage. For safety reasons public access to the building is not permitted.
By bus: 2, 50, 88, 155, 196, 333, 345, P5
By Tube: Stockwell

See also CAPTIONS TO IMAGES on pages 218–220

STOCKWELL BUS GARAGE, 1952

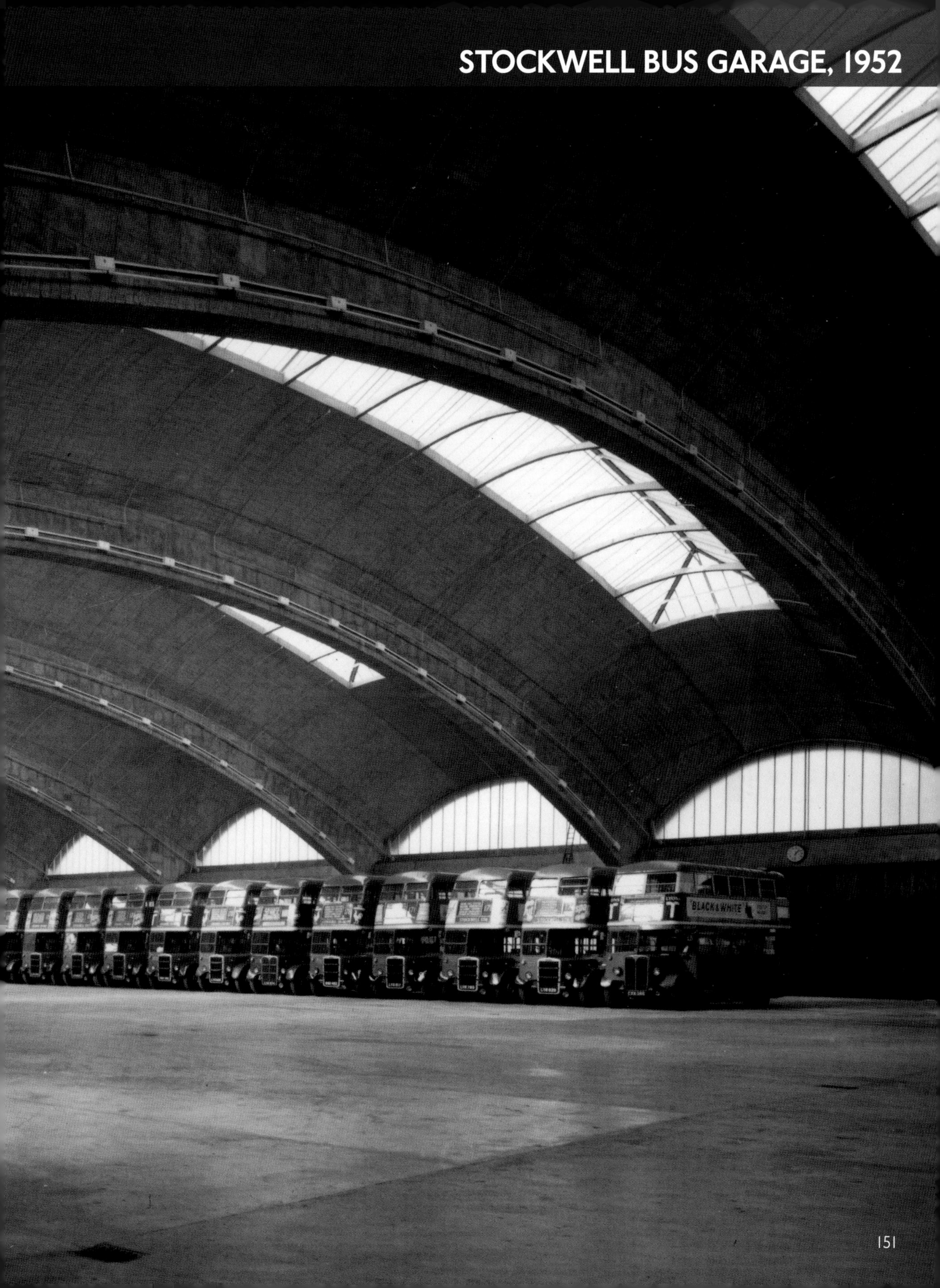

WHAT MAKES IT SPECIAL

*'These bus maps are invaluable
for users of this essential service.'*

CURATOR'S NOTES

In 2014, Transport for London designed
a night bus services map with a dark blue
background to sit alongside the daytime
bus map (which is white). Like the Night
Tube map, the bus version has to convey
the message of differing route and service
standards as clearly as possible.

The night map has been tested in a new
material (polypropylene) to increase
product life expectancy, reduce
maintenance costs and improve customer
presentation. The latest versions also
feature the elegant redesigned night
owl symbol.

WHERE TO SEE IT

Some bus shelters in central
London and the suburbs

'At a time when there was no contactless, no Oyster and no zones, these ticket machines helped to provide some clarity to customers … I wish we still had some of these on the network today, updated for today's common fares.'

CURATOR'S NOTES

Although their styling might suggest 1950s or 1960s manufacture, these ticket machines, produced by Brecknell, Munro & Rogers, were quietly futuristic. They first appeared in busy Underground stations as early as 1937.

At that time, individual tickets were purchased from one point to another, many with different prices. These clearly labelled machines helped regular commuters buy tickets for commonly made journeys that cost a set amount – on the poster, it shows 4d. They were both functional and beautiful.

They were still in use at some locations into the 1980s.

WHERE TO SEE IT
Museum Depot

See also CAPTIONS TO IMAGES on pages 218–220

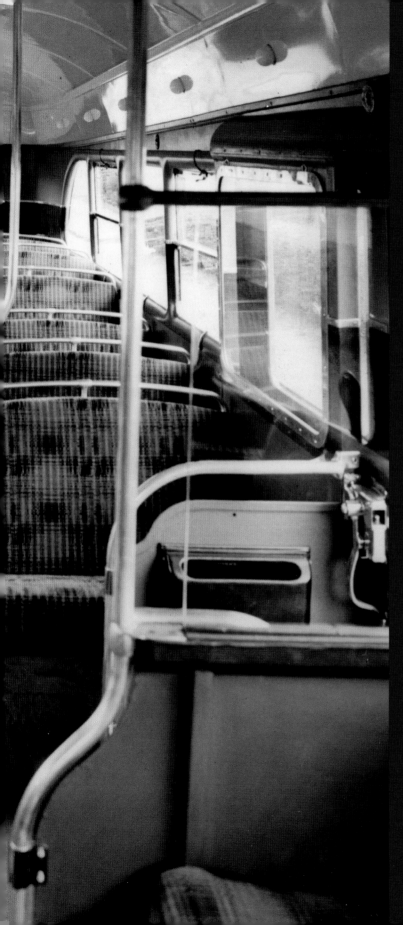

'This design set a standard of form liberated from function ... one of my favourite buses.'

CURATOR'S NOTES

First introduced in 1935, the Q type bus was a revolutionary design, years ahead of its time. Its engine is mounted under the floor behind the driver, which meant that it could be built without the usual bonnet at the front. This allowed graceful curves and a form that was not dictated by the mechanics of the vehicle.

WHERE TO SEE IT

Museum Depot

See also CAPTIONS TO IMAGES on pages 218–220

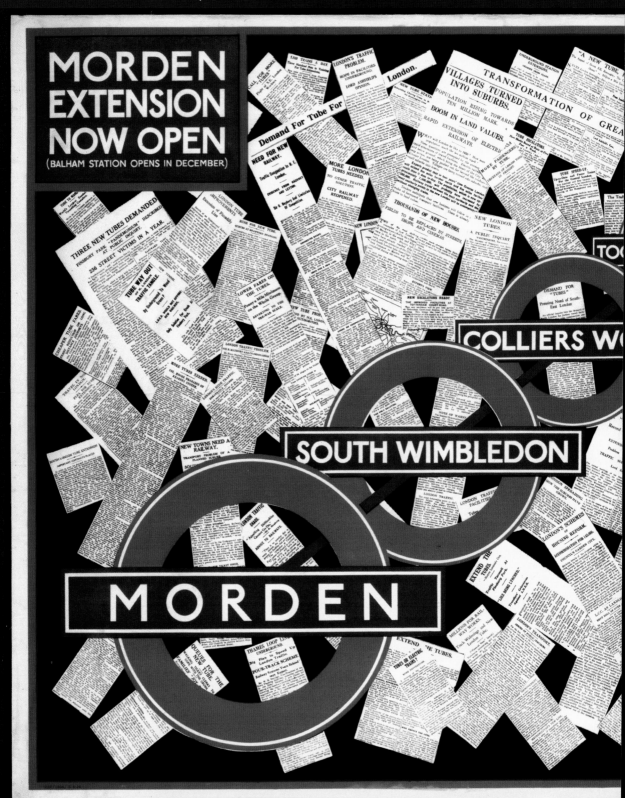

The large front windows let light into the stations, bringing a sense of sunshine into the darkness of the Underground. And at night, when the stations are lit up, the glow from these windows appears as a beacon to weary travellers making their way home.'

CURATOR'S NOTES

Frank Pick commissioned architect Charles Holden to design eight new stations for the Northern line extension, southwest from Clapham to Morden. Holden designed adaptable frontages with three sections that could be flat, set back or bent to fit corner sites. The frontages gave each station a resemblance of form, imparting a unified style that could be customised to each site. Work began on the stations in 1924, and they opened in 1926 to great acclaim. The architecture of the stations is little changed today.

WHERE TO SEE IT

Northern line (Stockwell to Morden)
By bus: Numerous bus routes
By Tube: Northern line

See also CAPTIONS TO IMAGES on pages 218–220

RAINBOW INDICATOR BOARDS, 2006

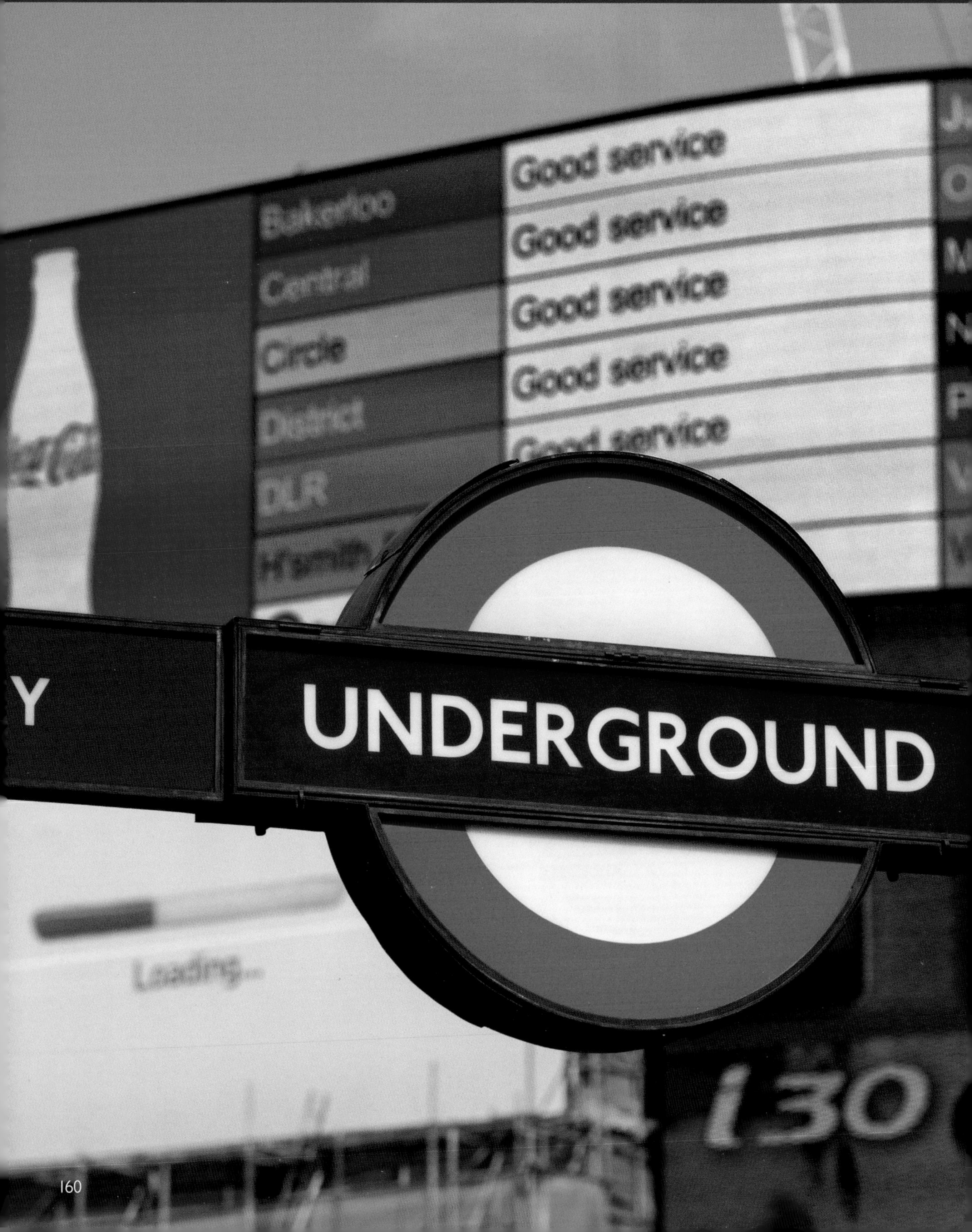

Good service
Good service
Good service
Good service
Good service
Good service
Good service

PUBLIC SUBWAY

'The rainbow indicator boards are a vibrant way to share customer information. It's easy to see at a glance what the service is like on the Underground and Overground, which is important on a complicated network like the one run by TfL.'

CURATOR'S NOTES

Rainbow indicator boards are located in most Tube stations, and are a simple and effective way of communicating the service status of Underground and Overground lines. The highly visible innovation was introduced in 2006 by Tim O'Toole, Managing Director of the Underground at the time. The initiative was accompanied by positive announcements such as, 'The Underground is running a good service on all lines'.

WHERE TO SEE IT

At stations across the Tube network

WHAT MAKES IT SPECIAL

'While we now have digital-based mechanisms like Trackernet that allow us to monitor train movement, none is as elegant as the housing mechanism for these dials.'

CURATOR'S NOTES

The service regulator dials installed in the reception area of 55 Broadway – the newly opened headquarters of the Underground Electric Railways Company of London (UERL) – showed the frequency of trains on each of the six lines then running. Senior managers passing by could consequently tell if the trains were running on time. The dials are practical but also stylish, and a similar style of indicator was installed at Piccadilly Circus. Although no longer functioning, the dials still give an audible 'thunk' every now and again.

WHERE TO SEE IT

55 Broadway, London SW1H 0BD
As the building is still occupied by Transport for London, public access to the interior is restricted.
By bus: 11, 24, 148, 211 to New Scotland Yard, then a short walk
By Tube: St James's Park

ACCESSIBLE BUS NETWORK, 1994

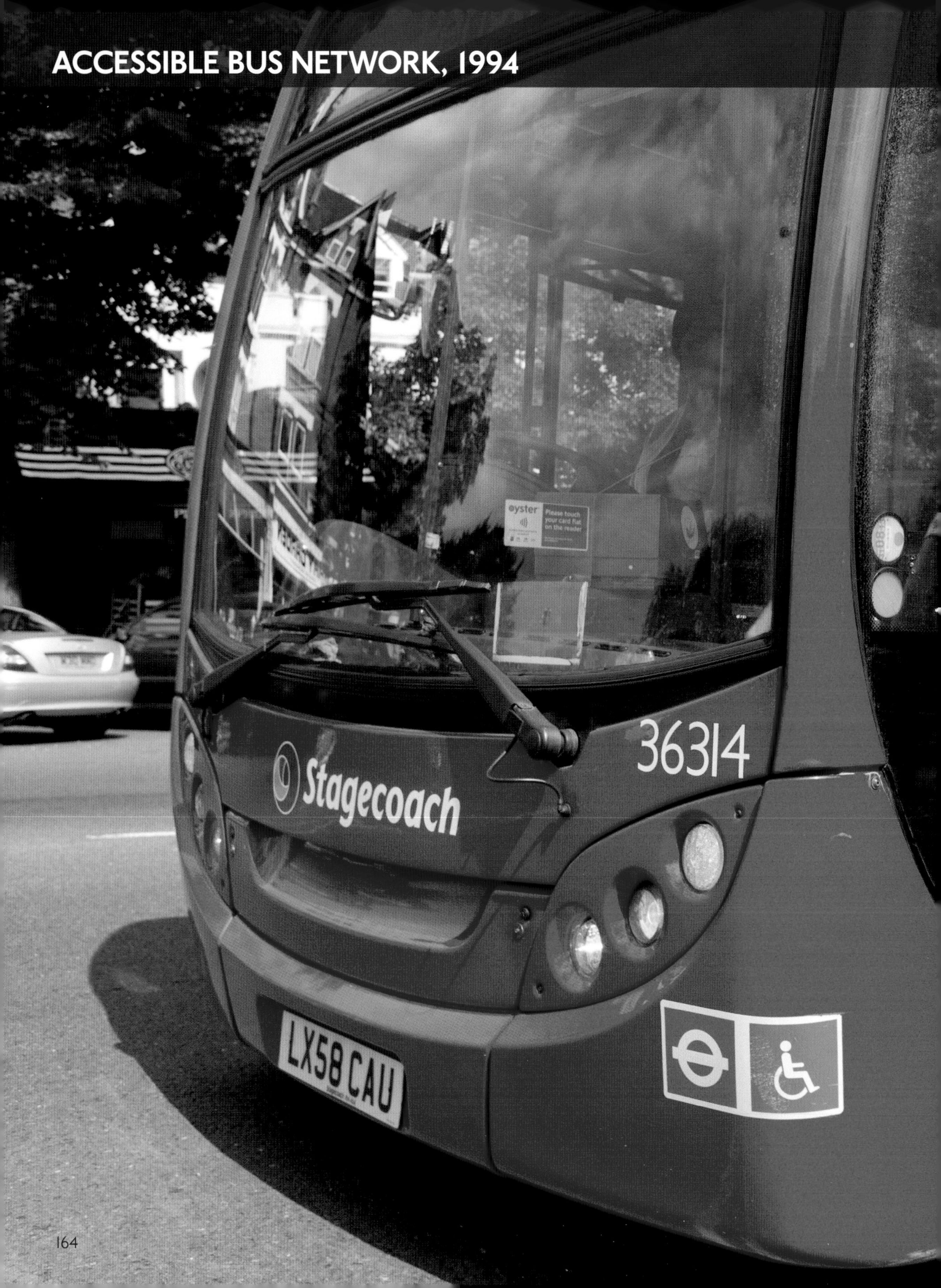

'Having a fully accessible bus network means that anyone can use the services safely and easily.'

CURATOR'S NOTES

Accessible low-floor buses were introduced experimentally in 1993 and came into service in 1994. They were designed to a specification drawn up by London Buses Ltd. In 2016, all 8,700 buses in Transport for London's modern fleet are low-floor and fitted with ramps, making them wheelchair accessible.

Access for disabled people, the elderly and parents with young children is a key issue in public transport. As well as accessible low-floor buses, design improvements include high contrast handrails for people with visual impairments, and on-board audible and visual announcements (iBus) to assist passengers who have sight and hearing loss.

The accessible bus network also includes bus stops. This means the kerb must be high enough for the wheelchair ramp to deploy, and for the step into the bus to be at a reasonable height. It also incorporates a protected 'clearway' that is free from any street furniture blocking access to the doors.

WHERE TO SEE IT

Every bus in London is accessible, except heritage Routemasters on route 15.

WHAT MAKES IT SPECIAL

'Introduced in 1910 when most buses were still horse-drawn, it really was the Routemaster bus of its day.'

CURATOR'S NOTES

The B type is remarkable for being the first reliable, mass-produced London bus. In 1908 the London General Omnibus Company (LGOC), the largest bus company in London at the time, merged with two of its leading rivals. Frank Searle, the LGOC's Chief Engineer, realised that London's traffic conditions required a vehicle of rugged design to withstand frequent stopping and starting.

The first design was the X type, a 34-seat double-decker, introduced in 1909. Further developments resulted in the B type in 1910, built at the LGOC works in Walthamstow using mass-production techniques. It was relatively quiet, reliable and easily maintained, and by 1913, some 2,500 had entered service.

WHERE TO SEE IT

London Transport Museum

See also CAPTIONS TO IMAGES on pages 218–220

'These buses perfectly encapsulate the social benefit of transportation, providing a lifeline for London residents who cannot use regular transport, allowing them to retain their independence.'

CURATOR'S NOTES

Improving access is a key consideration for all new transport schemes. London already has the world's largest fleet of accessible buses, with some 8,700 vehicles. Among Transport for London's many responsibilities is Dial-a-Ride. Operating since the 1980s, it is a supplementary service to the mainstream network, providing door-to-door transport for people with mobility issues.

The minibus vehicles are equipped to carry wheelchairs and are available by appointment. Dial-a-Ride has a fleet of 370 purpose-built vehicles that feature tip and fold seats to allow wheelchair users to manoeuvre around the vehicle more easily, and the buses provide greater flexibility for individual passengers' needs.

WHERE TO SEE IT

Operates all over London

WHAT MAKES IT SPECIAL

'Transport for London and its predecessors are noted world leaders in the provision of maps and service information for their customers.'

CURATOR'S NOTES

In the 1950s and 1960s a long-running and very elegant series of maps was produced for bus, Green Line, Underground and general London information. The simplicity and consistency of design for each mode was noteworthy and very satisfactory to the eye. Mapping content was also done to a very high (for the time) graphic standard.

WHERE TO SEE IT

London Transport Museum

See also CAPTIONS TO IMAGES on pages 218–220

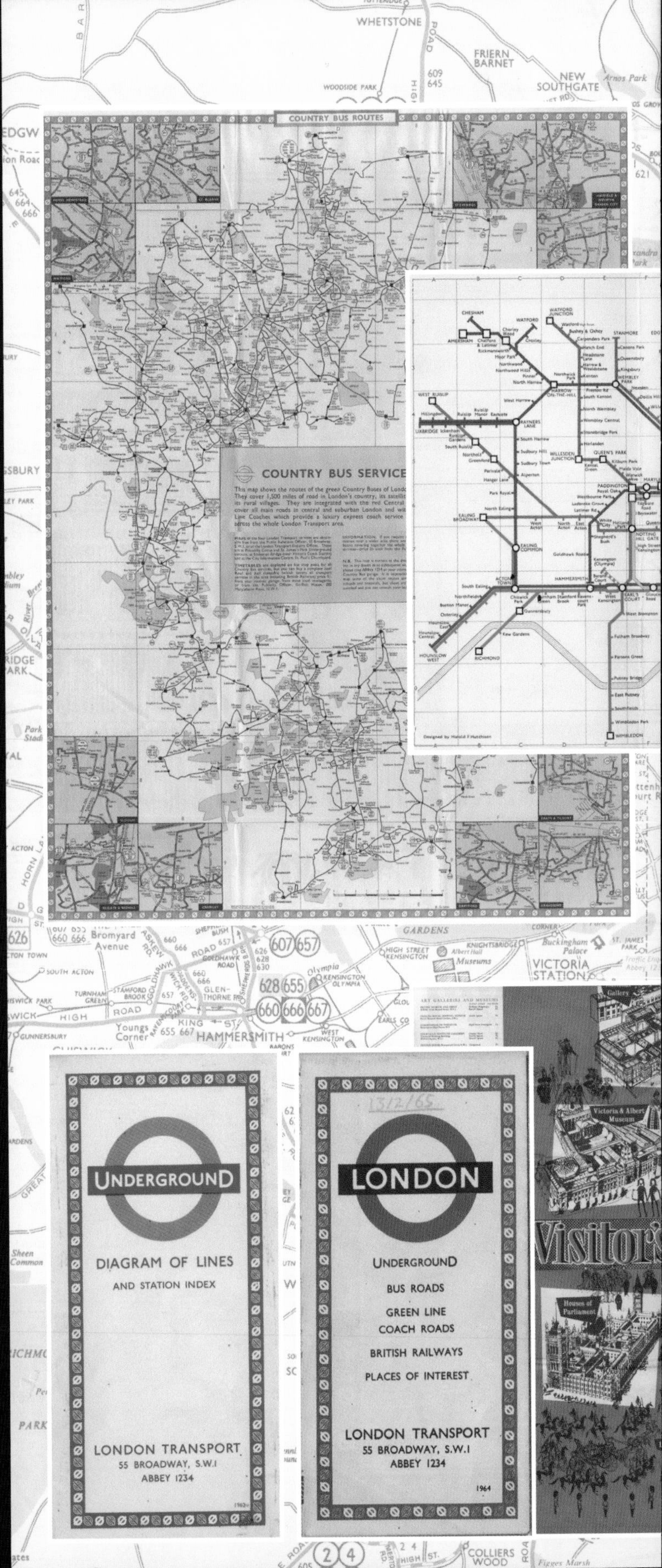

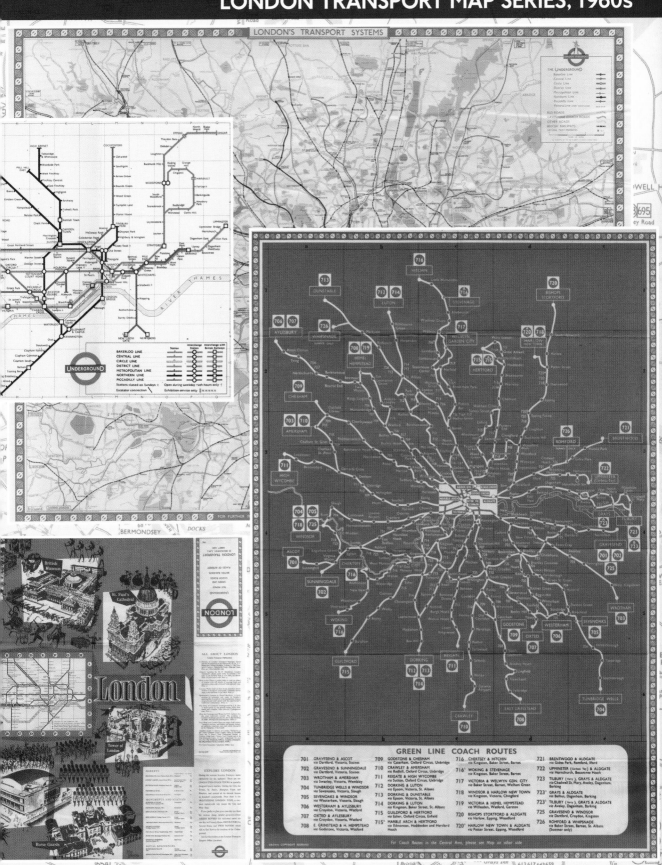

GREEN LINE COACH ROUTES

701 GRAVESEND & ASCOT	709 GODSTONE & CHESHAM	716 CHERTSEY & HITCHIN
via Dartford, Victoria, Staines	via Caterham, Oxford Circus, Uxbridge	via Kingston, Baker Street, Barnet
702 GRAVESEND & SUNNINGDALE	710 CRAWLEY & AMERSHAM	716ᵃ WOKING & STEVENAGE
via Dartford, Victoria, Staines	via Redhill, Oxford Circus, Uxbridge	via Kingston, Baker Street, Barnet
703 WROTHAM & AMERSHAM	711 REIGATE & HIGH WYCOMBE	717 VICTORIA & WELWYN GDN. CITY
via Swanley, Victoria, Wembley	via Sutton, Oxford Circus, Uxbridge	via Baker Street, Barnet, Welham Green
704 TUNBRIDGE WELLS & WINDSOR	712 DORKING & LUTON	718 WINDSOR & HARLOW NEW TOWN
via Sevenoaks, Victoria, Slough	via Epsom, Victoria, St. Albans	via Kingston, Victoria, Chingford
705 SEVENOAKS & WINDSOR	713 DORKING & DUNSTABLE	719 VICTORIA & HEMEL HEMPSTEAD
via Westerham, Victoria, Slough	via Epsom, Victoria, St. Albans	via Willesden, Watford, Garston
706 WESTERHAM & AYLESBURY	714 DORKING & LUTON	720 BISHOPS STORTFORD & ALDGATE
via Croydon, Victoria, Watford	via Kingston, Baker Street, St. Albans	via Harlow, Epping, Woodford
707 OXTED & AYLESBURY	715 GUILDFORD & HERTFORD	720ᵃ HARLOW NEW TOWN & ALDGATE
via Croydon, Victoria, Watford	via Esher, Oxford Circus, Enfield	via Potter Street, Epping, Woodford
708 E. GRINSTEAD & H. HEMPSTEAD	715ᵃ MARBLE ARCH & HERTFORD	
via Godstone, Victoria, Watford	via Edmonton, Hoddesdon and Hertford	
	Heath	

721 BRENTWOOD & ALDGATE
via Gidea Park, Romford, Ilford
722 UPMINSTER (Corner Toy) & ALDGATE
via Hornchurch, Becontree Heath
723 TILBURY (ferry), GRAYS & ALDGATE
via Chadwell St. Mary, Aveley, Dagenham, Barking
723ᵃ GRAYS & ALDGATE
via Belhus, Dagenham, Barking
723ᵇ TILBURY (ferry), GRAYS & ALDGATE
via Aveley, Dagenham, Barking
725 GRAVESEND & WINDSOR
via Dartford, Croydon, Kingston
726 ROMFORD & WHIPSNADE
via Baker Street, Barnet, St. Albans
(Summer only)

For Coach Routes in the Central Area, please see Map on other side

WHAT MAKES IT SPECIAL

'Exhibition Road demonstrates how streetscape design complements iconic architecture, how vehicles and pedestrians can interact and how materials can be used to their best effect.'

CURATOR'S NOTES

Exhibition Road is home to some of Britain's leading museums and institutions. For several years the Mayor of London, the Royal Borough of Kensington & Chelsea, and Westminster City Council worked jointly on proposals to improve the environment of the area. In 2011 the RIBA Award-winning Exhibition Road redevelopment was unveiled. Designed by architects Dixon Jones Ltd, the area was transformed from a space dominated by traffic, and with narrow, crowded pavements, into a 'shared space' where pedestrians and vehicles coexist equally.

WHERE TO SEE IT

Exhibition Road, London SW7
By bus: 9, 10, 14, 52, 74, 360, 414, 452, C1
By Tube: South Kensington

WHAT MAKES IT SPECIAL

'The requirement for passengers (and passers-by) to shelter and sit is done in a wholly integrated fashion.'

CURATOR'S NOTES

The 'mushroom shelter' at Oakwood station (named Enfield West from 1933 to 1946) was designed by Charles Holloway James, with Adams, Holden & Pearson as consulting architects. The shelter first appeared in 1933 at this station, and at Southgate and Turnpike Lane; also at Queensbury in 1935. Making subtle use of materials (concrete, timber and bronze) found within the station, the architecture is beautifully proportioned, with even the circumference of the shelter roof being picked out in a bronze strip within the terrazzo flooring and paving. The shelters, with their halo of lights, are stylish but also practical, providing cover for travellers.

WHERE TO SEE IT

Oakwood station
By bus: 121, 299, 307, 377
By Tube: Oakwood

See also CAPTIONS TO IMAGES on pages 218–220

'A ground-breaking Modernist approach to railway design, which has become an integral part of our rich design history and continues to be cherished by thousands.'

CURATOR'S NOTES

Sudbury Town on the Piccadilly line was built as a prototype for a new generation of Underground surface stations. Designed by Charles Holden, the style drew on contemporary European work in urban transport. Holden dubbed it a 'brick box with a concrete lid', and the approach was repeated in many forms, including the striking drum shapes of Arnos Grove and Southgate. These stations have since been recognised as among the finest British commercial architecture of their time.

WHERE TO SEE IT

Sudbury Town station
By bus: 18, 92, 182, 204, 245, 487, H17
By Tube: **Sudbury Town**

See also CAPTIONS TO IMAGES on pages 218–220

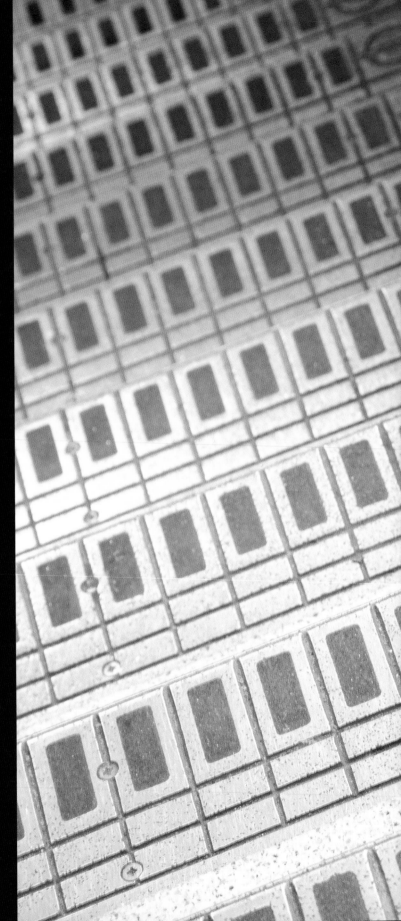

WHAT MAKES IT SPECIAL

'The step nosing across London Underground stations is, for me, a great example of an unseen, important element of the rich tapestry of design across Transport for London.'

CURATOR'S NOTES

Steel nosing to treads on staircases was used in the 1880s as a way of reducing wear and tear in high traffic areas at stations. In the 1950s a roundel was incorporated into the design.

The step nosing across London's Underground stations may go unnoticed by the millions of passengers who walk over it every day. However, with its embossed roundel, it is a design element that illustrates the great care and attention given to even the smallest detail.

WHERE TO SEE IT

On staircases all over the Tube network

WHAT MAKES IT SPECIAL

'*Like an enormous patchwork,*
Wrapper *tells the story of
the place in which it sits,
weaving together elements
from local history and the
natural environment, the area's
architecture and its people.*'

CURATOR'S NOTES

Wrapper is a permanent artwork by
Jacqueline Poncelet, commissioned
by Art on the Underground, that clads
the building and perimeter wall next to
Edgware Road (Circle line) station.

Created in vitreous enamel, *Wrapper*
dresses the building in a grid of patterns
which relate to different parts of the
local area. The colours reflect those of
the Tube map, hinting at the building's
connection to it. *Wrapper* can be seen
from many locations; from the Circle
line platform, on the surrounding streets,
and driving along the Marylebone Road.
Wrapper is the largest vitreous enamel
artwork in Europe.

WHERE TO SEE IT

Edgware Road station (Circle, District,
and Hammersmith & City)
By bus: 6, 7, 16, 18, 23, 27, 36, 98, 205,
332, 414, 436
By Tube: Edgware Road (Circle, District,
and Hammersmith & City)

VICTORIA LINE SIGNALLING BOX, c1968

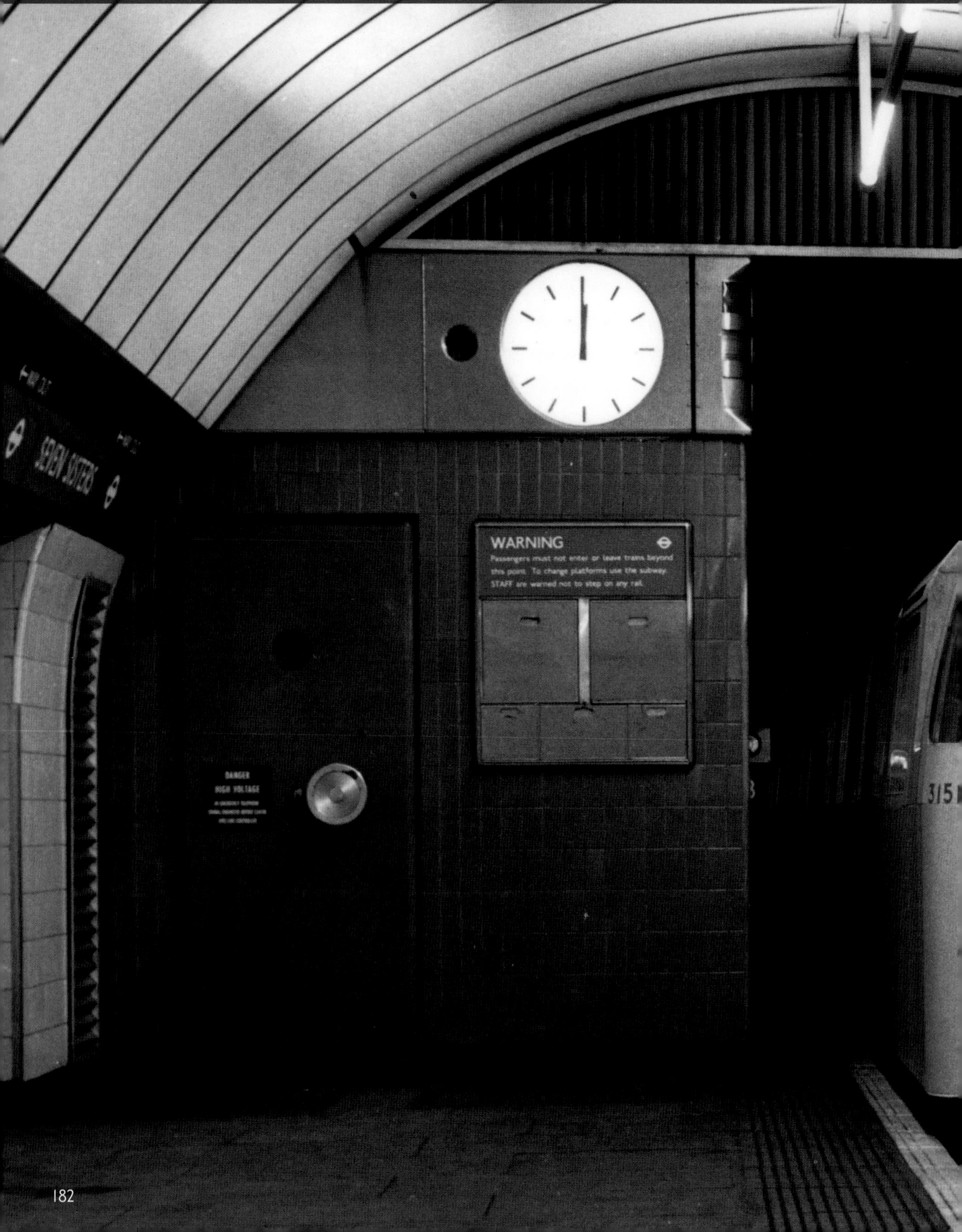

'This whole design made the driver's job easier, with a clear and uncluttered surface that had all the information needed.'

CURATOR'S NOTES

The Design Research Unit (DRU), a consultancy practice formed by Milner Gray, Misha Black and others, was responsible for the aesthetic style of the Victoria line, which opened between 1968 and 1972. Even the signalling equipment was designed to form part of the coordinated environment. The 'harbour light' signal (to the right of the clock) was so named because the glass lenses are reminiscent of marine lanterns. Made from brushed aluminium, it is typical of the Underground's architectural style during the 1960s.

WHERE TO SEE IT

London Transport Museum

See also CAPTIONS TO IMAGES on pages 218–220

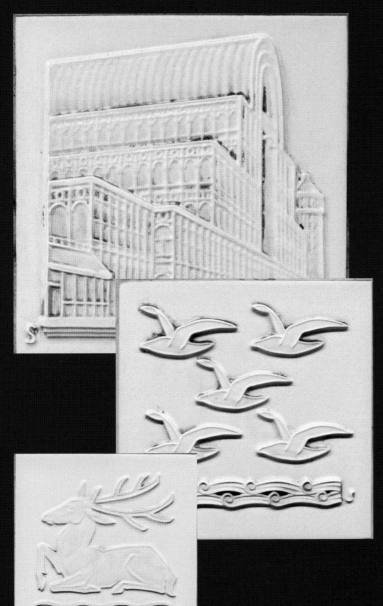

WHAT MAKES IT SPECIAL

'These tiles capture the care that was put into the design of some of the 1930s New Works Programme stations.'

CURATOR'S NOTES

Press-moulded tiles designed by Harold Stabler and made at Poole Pottery were used from 1938 to decorate platforms and concourses of new and refurbished stations, including Aldgate East, Bethnal Green, St John's Wood, St Paul's and Swiss Cottage. They represent the counties around London, plus symbols, buildings and historical figures associated with the city. There are 18 different designs, but only Swiss Cottage has the whole set.

Harold Stabler was closely associated with Frank Pick. As well as these tiles, he designed a company seal, a cap badge, bus radiator mascots and station platform ventilation grilles. He also designed many posters for London Transport and the Underground Group.

WHERE TO SEE IT

Swiss Cottage station
By bus: 13, 31, 46, 82, 113, 187, 268, C11
By Tube: Swiss Cottage

See also CAPTIONS TO IMAGES on pages 218–220

WHAT MAKES IT SPECIAL

'Only one of these was ever built, as an experiment. The tram is incredibly utilitarian, and it was designed as an attempt to lift the status of trams both aesthetically and from an engineering standpoint. The design helped the tram to run faster and improved the customer experience.'

CURATOR'S NOTES

The prototype Bluebird tram was the London County Council Tramways (LCCT) answer to London United Tramways' luxurious Feltham tram. Like its inspiration, Bluebird had an all-steel body, air doors and brakes, and a high standard of interior comfort and finish. But when the LCC tram services were taken over by London Transport, no further examples were built. It became the last tram made for service in London. Ultimately, the design was no match for the perceived benefits of the more flexible trolleybus, which replaced trams in the 1950s.

WHERE TO SEE IT

Bluebird tram No. 1 is preserved at the National Tramway Museum, Crich, in Derbyshire.

London Transport Museum has a model of the Bluebird tram.

See also CAPTIONS TO IMAGES on pages 218–220

'Bus advertising was introduced on the upper deck of horse-drawn buses in the 1860s, and continues today. It's an iconic part of London's transport history.'

CURATOR'S NOTES

Panels advertising bus company names and stopping points, or commercial products such as Pears soap, were first seen in the 1860s, at a time when riding on the top of a bus was a precarious affair. Access was via rungs on the back of the vehicle, which remained in use until replaced by proper staircases in the 1870s.

Advertising has always been an important source of revenue for London's bus companies. Enamel advertising plates covered most of the available space on the horse buses and early motorbuses, including the risers of the staircase on the back. Transparent adverts covered the narrow windows, and smaller bills were pasted inside.

WHERE TO SEE IT

London Transport Museum

See also CAPTIONS TO IMAGES on pages 218–220

SUDBURY T

'This is an example of the serif version of the Johnston font as used at Sudbury Town station. I particularly like this as it is a quirky version of the one that has evolved into the versatile and wholly recognisable New Johnston font used on all parts of our networks today.'

CURATOR'S NOTES

This font is a 'petit-serif' variation of Edward Johnston's alphabet. It was designed in the 1920s by Percy Delf Smith, a former pupil of Johnston. The typeface was created for use in the new London Transport headquarters building at 55 Broadway, and the architect Charles Holden contributed to the typeface as well. Holden also used it in several of the new stations on the Piccadilly line, notably at Sudbury Town (1931) and Arnos Grove (1932).

WHERE TO SEE IT

Sudbury Town station
By bus: 18, 92, 182, 204, 245, 487, H17
By Tube: Sudbury Town

WHAT MAKES IT SPECIAL

'This poster, by one of the most prolific and influential graphic designers of the 20th century, is one I admire greatly, as it strongly illustrates the often avant-garde nature of the artworks commissioned by the Underground. The bold geometric shapes of the clenched hand and the mechanical background create a striking, strong and exciting image, which was very much of its time.'

CURATOR'S NOTES

Edward McKnight Kauffer's poster, which features the massive Lots Road power station in the background, celebrates the advanced technology of the Tube. The bold and striking image not only emphasises the technological progression of the time, it also illustrates the Underground's confidence in modern design as a means of communication.

The geometric design suggests the influence of Futurism and the Art Deco style, and shows how Kauffer successfully introduced new styles of art to popular culture.

WHERE TO SEE IT
London Transport Museum

See also CAPTIONS TO IMAGES on pages 218—220

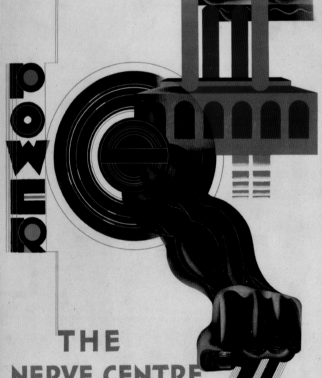

WHAT MAKES IT SPECIAL

'… stations were built over many years by different operating companies with different types of trains. Today the challenge is one of developing design fixes to address the engineering decisions made a century ago – particularly where accessibility is concerned. One such design … is the 'Up Down Ramp', a solution to the problems of varying platform heights at Underground stations.'

CURATOR'S NOTES

On a single journey passengers might step up to get off a train at one station, and step down to get off at another. Previously, ramps enabled wheelchair users to board only trains that were higher than the platform edge. The 'Up Down Ramp' can be used in either situation, increasing the number of stations that are accessible to wheelchair users. Parked on the platform, the ramp goes unnoticed by most of our customers, but it represents the continuing work being done to make the system accessible to as many passengers as possible.

WHERE TO SEE IT

Underground stations where the train floor is below platform level (Kilburn, Stanmore, Wembley Park, and 13 other stations across the network).

WHAT MAKES IT SPECIAL

'The rabbit, commonly known as "Wilfred the bunny", was originally intended to be fitted on the radiators of buses that served country areas.'

CURATOR'S NOTES

Animal mascots for motor vehicles became popular in the 1920s. The London General Omnibus Company (LGOC) took up the idea and commissioned a rabbit mascot for use on the radiator caps to promote their country bus services. Designed by the silversmith Harold Stabler and made in cast aluminium by the company Coan, it was originally intended to be 10cm (4in) high, but was increased to 20cm (8in) to have more impact. The pottery company Carter, Stabler & Adams produced presentation ceramic versions of the rabbit in 1922, to give to LGOC directors and other individuals.

The mascot acquired its nickname because of a resemblance to the long-eared rabbit called Wilfred who starred in the popular post-war *Daily Mirror* strip cartoon, 'Pip, Squeak and Wilfred'.

WHERE TO SEE IT
Museum Depot

See also CAPTIONS TO IMAGES on pages 218–220

'It is a reminder that the Metropolitan line was, and still is, more of a suburban railway. The coat of arms is elegant … I like it.'

CURATOR'S NOTES

The Metropolitan Railway's coat of arms bears the shield of the City of London (top left) and the counties it served – Middlesex (top right), Buckinghamshire (bottom left) and Hertfordshire (bottom right). The clenched fist with sparks at the top celebrates the power and capability of electric traction.

The symbolic coats of arms of the City of London's guilds and livery companies set a standard for the way in which many of London's companies, including its transport operators, chose to present their corporate identity.

WHERE TO SEE IT

London Transport Museum
Metropolitan Railway carriage

Museum Depot
Metropolitan Railway Milk Van
Carriage 353

See also CAPTIONS TO IMAGES on pages 218–220

WHAT MAKES IT SPECIAL

'The London Underground has a rich history of commissioning leading graphic designers and illustrators to create beautiful posters that communicate clear messages. I like the vibrant and optimistic posters from the post-war period and beyond. One favourite is the Cut Travelling Time poster of 1969 by Eckersley, which manages to be both clever and straightforward.'

CURATOR'S NOTES

Tom Eckersley was trained at Salford College of Art and, with fellow student Eric Lombers, formed an artistic partnership that until 1939 produced innovative posters for many clients, including London Transport. Eckersley later became Head of Graphic Design at the prestigious London College of Printing, and he, together with Abram Games, was at the forefront of poster design in the period between 1950 and 1975. Both designers were frequently commissioned by London Transport.

WHERE TO SEE IT
Museum Depot

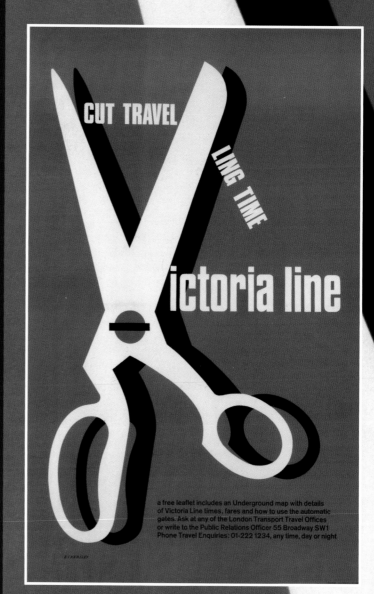

See also CAPTIONS TO IMAGES on pages 218–220

Victoria

LIFT GRILLES BY LESLIE GREEN, 1906

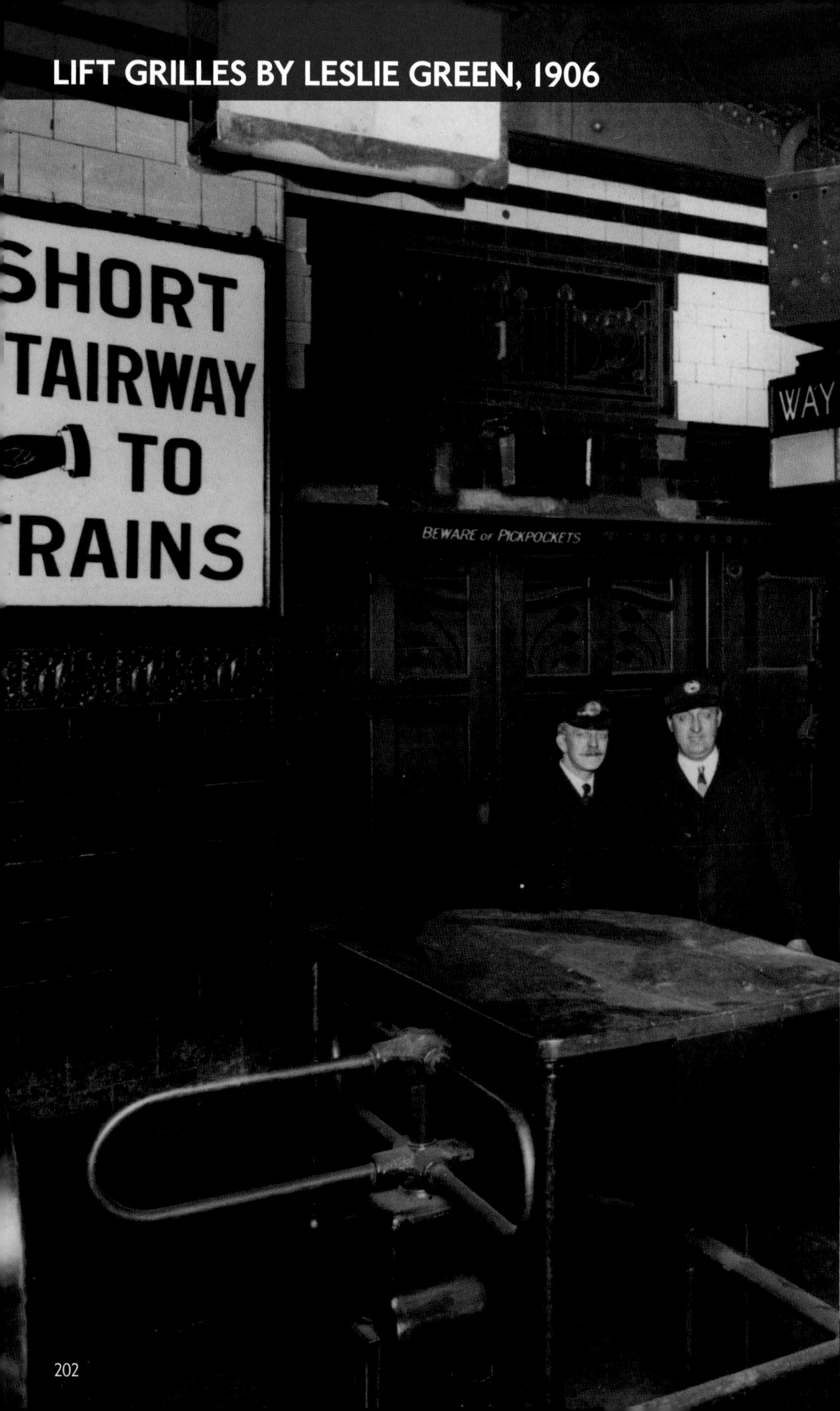

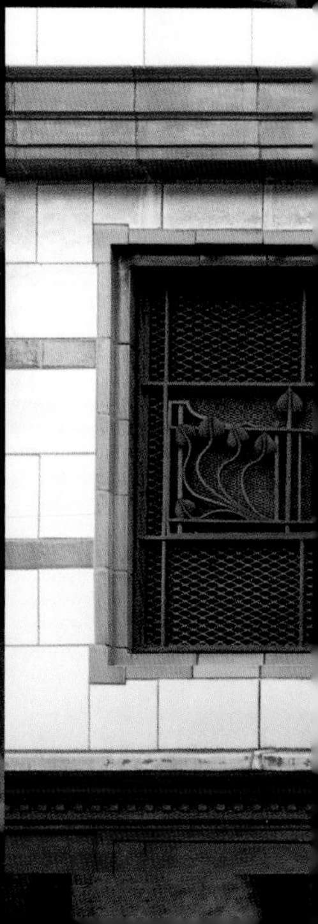

See also CAPTIONS TO IMAGES on pages 218–220

WHAT MAKES IT SPECIAL

'Like the rest of his station designs, Green approached lift design with care, adding beautiful wrought-iron details on a utilitarian object. He made the commute beautiful, and I wish more of these survived today.'

CURATOR'S NOTES

The stations designed by Leslie Green for the Underground Electric Railways Company of London (UERL) featured a number of Art Nouveau flourishes. This influence was evident in the ornamental use of decorative wrought iron on the lift shaft ventilation grilles. Lift shafts in the new stations had ventilation holes at the top and bottom of the lift doors. Instead of concealing them, Green applied curving, plant-like forms typical of the Art Nouveau style to the grilles, which also feature the lift car number.

WHERE TO SEE IT

Mornington Crescent station

Museum Depot

'As a piece of architecture, it is really exciting; it looks like some kind of stealth aircraft emerging from the Thames.'

CURATOR'S NOTES

Millbank Millennium Pier was opened in 2003, the last of a group of five new piers on the Thames funded by the Millennium Commission. Designed by Marks Barfield Architects, with a lighting installation by artist Angela Bulloch, the pier is served by the river route RB2, linking the Tate Britain and Tate Modern art galleries.

WHERE TO SEE IT

Millbank Millennium Pier
By river: River Bus RB2 St George Wharf – Millbank – Embankment – Bankside
By bus: 87
By Tube: Pimlico, then a short walk

WHAT MAKES IT SPECIAL

'West Acton station in the evening. Jewel-like architecture and a wonderful sight! I'd passed West Acton station many times without giving it very much thought, so it came as a surprise to suddenly discover the beauty of the architecture in the twilight with the yellow glow coming from the ticket office.'

CURATOR'S NOTES

Designed by the Great Western Railway architect Brian Lewis in the late 1930s, West Acton was intended to be the model that other rebuilt Central line stations would follow, but the programme was interrupted by the onset of the Second World War.

WHERE TO SEE IT

West Acton station
By bus: 440
By Tube: West Acton

WHAT MAKES IT SPECIAL

Windrush Square is a great example of the crossover between transport infrastructure, transport interchange, public space and community asset.'

CURATOR'S NOTES

Transport for London's Urban Design team works with the Greater London Authority and London boroughs to create attractive and well-connected streets and places. Windrush Square in Brixton, in the London Borough of Lambeth, opened in February 2010. It was designed by the landscape architects GROSS MAX to reorganise three pre-existing open spaces – Tate Gardens, St Matthew's Gardens and the original grassy Windrush Square – into one pedestrianised park and square. The £8.7m project was part of TfL's broader Brixton Town Centre Improvement scheme, completed later in 2010.

Windrush Square has changed a once over-congested interchange space into an asset that can be used by the whole community.

WHERE TO SEE IT

Windrush Square, Brixton Hill, SW2
By bus: 2, 3, 35, 37, 45, 59, 109, 118, 133, 159, 196, 250, 322, 333, 345, 355, 415, 432, P4, P5
By Tube: Brixton

'This stylish bridge was built to do an important job, relieving congestion in west London.'

CURATOR'S NOTES

The A316 road is a principal route from London to southwest England, built between the First and Second World Wars to relieve pressure on the narrow and overcrowded Hammersmith and Richmond bridges and connecting road networks.

Chiswick Bridge is one of the two bridges (the other is Twickenham) over the River Thames on the relief road. Constructed mainly of concrete with Portland stone facing, the bridge was designed by the architect Sir Herbert Baker and the Middlesex County Engineer Alfred Dryland.

This elegant Grade II listed structure was strengthened and refurbished in 2015, and still carries many thousands of vehicles every day. It is also a key vantage point for the annual Boat Race between the universities of Oxford and Cambridge, a fixture since 1829.

WHERE TO SEE IT

Chiswick Bridge, W4
By bus: 190
By river: Seasonal river services

DESIGN PHILOSOPHY AT TRANSPORT FOR LONDON

Q & A with Jon Hunter,
Head of Design at Transport for London

Good design presents solutions to a multitude of situations and problems. How has the approach to design solutions for transport evolved over the last century?

London Transport and Transport for London (TfL) evolved to reflect the changing priorities and scope of the organisation as it expanded, and as the city grew. This said, the fundamental design philosophy of balancing form, function and cost has remained omnipresent – the ever-moving sliders on this equation provide a constant challenge in ensuring both design intent and translation is constant.

When Londoners think of TfL, they may not immediately think of design. How central is the design team to everyday life at TfL HQ?

Design is integral to everything that we do as an organisation, in the same way as it touches every aspect of our everyday lives. We have an extraordinary heritage of placing design at the forefront of our thinking, and although we have differing priorities in these austere times in 2016, design is still very much embedded in everything we do – sweating the details with our feet to the fire, championing the importance and fiscal value that intelligent design brings to the organisation.

There have been some wonderful artistic collaborations on transport design over the years, from Man Ray to Paolozzi. What are the intentions and inspirations behind these collaborations?

It is within our very DNA to bring excellence to all that we do, whether it is designing a new bus or creating a memorable piece of new publicity. We take pride in recognising and commissioning the greatest design leaders of the time – including contemporary counterparts such as Barber & Osgerby (design partner for Crossrail trains), Thomas Heatherwick (New Routemaster bus), Mark Wallinger (*Labyrinth* artworks for Art on the Underground) and Paul Catherall (original posters of iconic London architecture) – to name but a few. They represent the cultural essence of our time in a way that speaks to present and future generations.

London is often thought to be a world leader in art and culture. Would you say this is the same for our transport system? Do other cities follow our lead?

One need only look at how our iconic Tube map has been emulated around the world to see the learning drawn from our design into other metropolises. The rapid integration of contactless payment into everyday life is another example. This is not to say that we can stand still; we constantly need to look at how we can make things even better for our customers — while balancing a rapidly transforming, and increasingly complex, integrated network.

What message is TfL trying to deliver? How would you like Londoners and tourists to feel as they go about daily life using the city's transport system?

A simple one. That 'Every Journey Matters', and I strive to reach the day when all of our customers view our system as the invisible enabler to everything that they do, providing reliable, quick and easy connections to help them through the day.

So, as an 'invisible enabler', should good transport design be standout or systemic — blending into the fabric of a well-run system?

Integration of design into the wider context is important, but never by compromising functionality — design should be both beautiful but also hard-working, ensuring simplicity and accessibility.

What would you say is the most standout transport design icon of the last 100 years?

For me, it is the one that is rarely noticed and constantly serves — the signage that guides our users around our system with such graceful ease and cognitive simplicity.

In 2015, Transport for London (TfL) and London Transport Museum launched Transported by Design, a programme of events and activities showcasing the innovative ways good design is used in today's transport network and how this keeps London working and growing.

As part of the programme we invited the public to vote for their favourite design icons, drawn from London's extensive transport history and the modern-day network.

People were asked to vote from a shortlist of 100 transport design icons that had been carefully selected by industry experts, TfL and London Transport Museum staff. A wide spectrum of London's transport designs were on the list, including the uplighters at St John's Wood Underground station, moquette seating and the 'Push once' bus bell – as well as more modern designs like the cable car and Cycle Hire bikes.

The top ten icons were announced – including the classic black taxi, the world famous Tube map and the ever-recognisable roundel. The enthusiasm behind the entire list was infectious and it seemed a shame to limit our celebrations to these icons, which is why this book has been produced to celebrate all the icons on the list.

We would like to thank all members of the public and TfL staff who took the time to highlight and vote for their favourite icons. Many of the submissions featured interesting and engaging reasons why they were beloved – particularly those from TfL staff, who work with many of these icons every day. Unfortunately we could not feature all of them in the book, but we have included a selection of the many we received.

TRANSPORTED BY DESIGN
SUPPORTED BY:

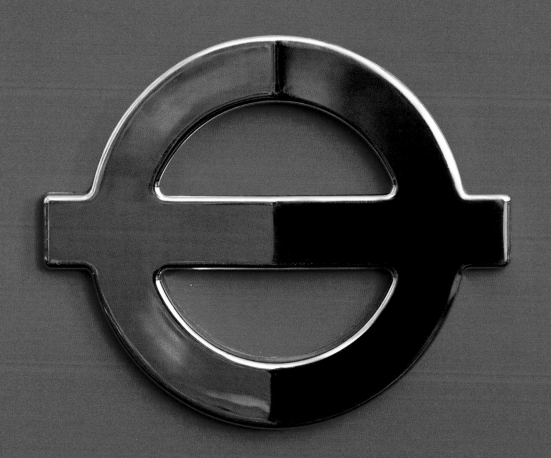

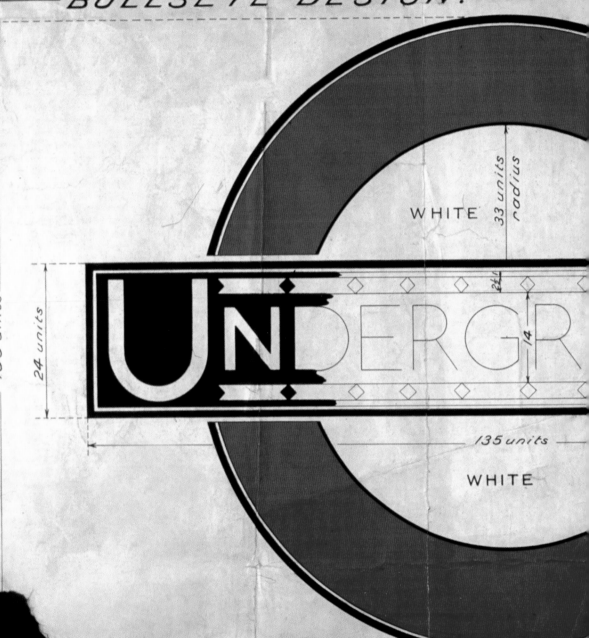

UNDERGROUND

PROPORTIONS OF STANDARD —— BULLSEYE DESIGN. ——

100 units

24 units

WHITE

33 units radius

WHITE

135 units

...ed design Nº 659,824 (if flat).
,,   Nº 659,822 (if any part in relief).

Standard "Underground" lettering,
copy of alphabet on application.
Large "U" & "D" 19 units high; 2½ thick;
remaining letters 10 units high, 1½".

White legend on
dark blue ground.

½ unit white
1 "   black
15 units bright red
½ unit black.

FILING ROOM

DRAWER No.

OFFICE OF THE SIGNAL ENGINEER
(Chief Engineer's Dept.)

Drg. No. B.L. 1372.

217

CAPTIONS TO IMAGES

The captions provide information and references (shown in brackets) for London Transport Museum images used in the book. Images sourced elsewhere are listed in the PICTURE CREDITS on page 221. To see more of the Museum's collections, including the photograph and poster collections, visit **ltmuseum.co.uk**

CAPTIONS TO IMAGES continued

Pages 156–157   Exterior view of the Museum's Q type single deck motor bus No. Q55 built by AEC in 1935. Photo by Hugh Robertson, 2001 (2002/17539).

Interior of a Q type country bus, by Topical Press, 1935 (1998/89024).

Pages 158–159   Poster featuring station roundels and news cuttings celebrating the 'new Tube' on the Northern line. Produced for the opening of the Morden extension in 1926 (1983/4/2131).

Pages 166–167   New LGOC B type buses on route 1, ready for service with their crews at Cricklewood bus garage, 1911 (1998/84482).

Pages 170–171   1960s maps featured include (clockwise from top left) Country bus services map; pocket Tube map; London Transport systems map; Green Line coach routes; *Visitor's London* guide; Underground pocket maps with decorative borders.

Pages 174–175   *Right:* Enfield West Underground station (now Oakwood) in 1933. The illuminated light mast shelter, introduced to mark the station's presence after dark, also incorporates a roundel. Photo by Topical Press (1998/88355).

Pages 176–177   Exterior of the reconstructed Sudbury Town station building with an ST type bus on the forecourt, by Topical Press, 1931 (1998/77011).

Pages 182–183   Tube train bound for Brixton entering the southbound Victoria line platform at Seven Sisters station by Colin Tait, 1974 (1998/65792).

Pages 184–185   The stylised designs featured are c1938 and show, *clockwise from top:*

Five princesses, representing Berkshire; the roundel, representing London Transport (1996/3500); Crystal Palace; five birds over water, representing the River Thames; a stag representing Hertfordshire; crown and three curved, notched swords representing Middlesex (1996/4192).

Pages 186–187   Experimental LCC 'Bluebird' tram No. 1 in service at Manor House, northeast London by Topical Press, 1932 (1998/87575).

Pages 188–189   A crowded LGOC Favorite 'knifeboard' horse bus, photo by Rhodes, c1865 (1998/83643).

Pages 192–193   This shows the final printed *Power* poster. The original artwork, which is in the Museum's collection, reveals how Kauffer's American spelling of 'center' was amended before printing (1983/4/2998).

Pages 196–197   Detail from a 1923 poster by Irene Fawkes advertising bus routes to the country. It features the Stabler rabbit mascot on the bonnet of the bus (1983/4/8308).

Cast bronze version of the rabbit mascot, mounted on a marble plinth, 1922. Presented to George Shave, Chief Engineer and Operating Manager of the LGOC (1993/43).

Pages 198–199   Metropolitan Railway steam locomotive No. 108, bound for Aylesbury, c1930 (1998/87438).

Pages 200–201   *Cut travelling time* poster for the Victoria line by Tom Eckersley, 1969. A blue version listed stations on the line. Many journey times were halved by the new, direct, cross-London links (1983/4/7729).

Pages 202–203   Trafalgar Square Underground station, by Topical Press, 1922. Colour inset shows the grilles at Mornington Crescent station (1998/89912).

Pages 216–217   Diagram showing the standard layout of the 'Registered Design' version of the Johnston roundel, c1925 (2000/9202)

PICTURE CREDITS

Many of the images reproduced in this book are from the London Transport Museum collection, © TfL. For more information see CAPTIONS TO IMAGES on pages 218–220.

Sources for all other images are listed alphabetically below, with page references.

Alamy Stock Photo / Zefrog: 66–67, 76–77

Art on the Underground: 92–93

Thierry Bal: 24–25 (photo details), 88–89 (*Sea Strata* artwork – photo detail), 180–181

HemingwayDesign: 134–135 (uniform design)

Dennis Gilbert: 30–31, 38–39

Ian Jones: 100–101 (colour photo)

David Mellor Studio: 132–133

Mini Moderns: 54–55 ('Push once' graphic)

Press Association / Chris Radburn: 76–77

M & C Saatchi: 52 (inset) poster design by M & C Saatchi, illustration by Rob Bailey

TfL Visual Services Archive: 12–13, 80–81 (top right), 88–89, 104–105, 123 (top), 208–209

TfL / Ian Bell: 42 (left), 94–95

TfL / Eleanor Bentall: 34–35

TfL / Rob Cadman: 130–131

TfL / Mike Garnett: 4, 28–29, 42–43, 46–47, 49 (middle), 52–53, 58–59, 64–65, 70–71, 84–85, 100, 108–109, 110, 124–125, 136–137, 148–149 (main image), 160–165, 178–179, 210–211, 215, 221, back cover (left)

TfL / Dave King: 134–135

TfL / Luca Marino: 45 (middle), 168–169, 206–207

TfL / Thomas Riggs: 21, 36–37 (excluding top left), 74, 82–83, 140–141, 144–145, 152–153, 174, 184–185, 194–195, 211 (aerial view)

TfL / Nick Turpin: 12, 106 (top), 135 (top)

TfL / Kris Wood: 203 (inset), 204–205